Barbara Griggs was for m........................r on the
London *Evenin*.......................ut her
interests as auth......................ng, and
she has written ....teenth-
century history, g.....................nutri-
tion and herbal ....has appeared in
most national dailies, and in leading magazines including
Harpers and Queen, *Cosmopolitan*, *New Health*, *Homes
and Gardens*, and *Mother*.

She is married to Henri van der Zee, London Corres-
pondent of the Dutch newspaper *De Telegraaf*, and they
have two daughters.

By the same author

Nouveau Poor, or How to Live Better on Less (with Shirley Lowe)
William and Mary (with Henri van der Zee)
A Sweet and Alien Land (with Henri van der Zee)
Green Pharmacy: A History of Herbal Medicine
The Home Herbal: A Handbook of Simple Remedies

BARBARA GRIGGS

Baby's Cookbook

PANTHER
Granada Publishing

Panther Books
Granada Publishing Ltd
8 Grafton Street, London W1X 3LA

Revised edition published by Panther Books 1979
2nd revised edition 1984
Reprinted 1985

First published in Great Britain as *Bibi's Cookbook* by
Allen & Unwin Ltd 1976

ISBN 0-583-12998-6

Printed and bound in Great Britain by
Collins, Glasgow

Set in Times

FOR BIBI
Without whom there would
have been no Cookbook

AND HENRI
Without whom there would
have been no Bibi

Contents

Acknowledgements

I acknowledge with gratitude the help given me by many kind girl-friends, who passed on recipes, advice and suggestions from their own experience of bringing up a family, or bravely tried out Bibi's favourites on their babies.

I should like to express my particular thanks to my husband Henri van der Zee, who first suggested the idea of this book, and encouraged me throughout by his interest and enthusiasm; to Miss Ineke Jager for all her patient field-work; to Helen O'Leary, professional super-cook, for technical advice and help; and first and last, to Bibi herself, most adorable and co-operative of guinea-pigs.

Author's Note

By long-standing tradition, the authors of baby-books almost invariably refer to babies – like God – as 'he', though Spock is at least gentleman enough to apologize for the practice.

In Bibi's honour I have flouted tradition, and babies are here referred to throughout as 'she'. But this doesn't of course mean that I am writing only for baby girls, any more than Spock writes only about little boys. I have not so far come across any significant difference between the palates of boy and girl babies, other than the quirks of taste we all have. And nutritionally the requirements of male and female babies are much the same – unless, of course, the boy is bigger, in which case presumably he is also hungrier, and needs more to eat.

Foreword

Cooking for a baby?

You mean – real cookery?

That was the sort of reaction I got from friends and colleagues a decade ago when they heard that my first daughter Bibi was getting home-cooking all the time once she'd started on solid food. They were incredulous. Why go to all that trouble, they wanted to know, when a modern mother simply didn't have to any more? Hadn't I heard about commercial baby foods?

Well, yes, I had. I also felt very strongly that I wanted my baby to have the best possible start in life, in every way. And how could pre-cooked, tinned, warmed-up bland commercial baby-food compare with fresh, tasty wholesome domestic home-cooking? Cookery, after all, is more than just another domestic chore, it's an act of creative caring, of love and concern for the people gathered round your table. Why should a baby be left out in the cold, fed from terrible jars and tins all the time?

I hope that mothers who share these views will find my book useful, practical and encouraging. But such mothers will, at least, have the comfort of knowing they are not an eccentric minority any more. For in those years, fortunately, attitudes to baby-diet have changed enormously. We are becoming, as a nation, more and more enthusiastic cooks, so it seems natural to cook for even the smallest member of the family. Thanks largely to the excellent job done by women's magazines, we all know much about the importance of diet in relation to our shape and health; and a new crop of magazines for mothers of small babies has also shown how to relate this knowledge to a baby's diet.

Other changes have taken place in those years. For a start, most of us are poorer than we used to be, and few women can now afford to feed their babies out of tins, jars and packets all the time, even if they wanted to. Rising prices have turned some cuts of meat and – sadly – many kinds of fish into luxuries for special occasions. If it weren't for chicken, some of us would already be vegetarians from sheer economic necessity. For this reason, although I've tried to give a wide range of suggestions for a baby's main meal, by no means all of them are for fish and meat, and even then they are mainly for the cheaper varieties. It hardly seems sensible these days to be buying little bits of meat just for a baby – especially when she can be just as well nourished on milk or cheese as on steak. So I've worked out lots of tasty egg, cheese and vegetable recipes for these non-meat meals; and almost all of these simple little dishes contain enough complete protein in the form of egg, milk, cheese or wheatgerm to make them a perfect nourishing meal for a baby. And for you too, if it comes to that.

If any reader should be kind enough to wonder how Bibi herself fared on this diet, I can say with my hand on my heart that both she and her younger sister Ninka are slim, lively, lovely exuberant creatures, with hearty appetites.

Introduction

In those distant days before we turned into a Family, planning meals simply meant thinking up something delicious to cook for the two of us for dinner. And then there were three of us. And then our darling daughter Bibi was into solid food. And in no time at all, it seemed, I was feverishly planning three mini-meals a day for her.

What is there that's good for a baby? And that she will like? And that doesn't need lots of teeth to cope with? And that she won't choke on? – the ever-present terror of first-time-round mothers. My mind used to go a total blank. If all the baby books didn't agree that three eggs a week is the limit for those early months, Bibi would probably have lived on eggs; I thought it the perfect convenience food for small babies. But that still left four eggless days a week – not to mention all those other meals.

There was no question, either, of doing what lots of baby books advised: simply feeding her a little of the family lunch, puréed to a suitable mushiness. My husband and I like our food rich, garlicky and highly seasoned – a bit much for a tiny baby. And weekends apart, the main meal eaten in our house – as in millions of other homes, I imagine – is in the evening. Warmed-up and mushed-up leftovers from last night weren't my idea of a sound baby diet.

So almost every mealtime, it seemed, was a new problem, and I was racked by doubt and indecision twice a day. Should she eat onions? Would she choke on the pips of a tomato? Was fish all right for a small baby? – I never seemed to have *heard* of people feeding fish to small babies, somehow. Was fresh fruit too acid for her? Was yogurt indigestible or something? Would potatoes make her fat? Did she *need* sugar? Was she getting enough protein?

Looking back now, I don't know whether to laugh at or be appalled by my total ignorance of nutrition.

But even if I had known everything I have since eagerly learned on the subject, that still wouldn't have saved me from the doubts, the panic, and the nerve-sapping diffidence which every first-time mother knows. We are so new to it all, few of us are lucky enough to have reliable family or friends around to whom we can turn in moments of crisis, and we are all absolutely terrified of doing the wrong thing – to the point where even the most level-headed of us tend to lose our cool and our common sense.

It is this diffidence, I believe, far more than mere convenience, that explains the overwhelming success of the commercial babyfood companies. They make it all sound so easy: their literature adorned with photographs of particularly lively, attractive and healthy-looking babies, is so benign and sympathetic in tone; their advice sounds so fearfully authoritative. And their propaganda, accompanied by a generous supply of free samples, is often delivered to young mums in hospital only days after baby is born – when women are pretty susceptible, to put it mildly. How can the nervous young mum of a precious first baby resist such blandishments – particularly when it means less work for her into the bargain, and is considered perfectly normal by all her friends? So normal, indeed, that it is the idea of producing fresh, wholesome, home-cooked food for your baby that today seems eccentric. In this matter, the degree to which a whole generation of young mothers has been successfully brainwashed is startling. I nearly fell for it all myself.

What saved Bibi from a whole babyhood of eating out of little jars and tins was my own pride. And my greed. I love to cook, I think that good food is one of the great blessings of civilization, and I wouldn't consider feeding family or friends out of jars and tins all the time. Why should my baby eat worse than any of us? – particularly since, as a busy working mother, I had full-time help with her in the shape of a young Dutch girl, Ineke Jager.

Ignorant though I was, too, about nutrition, I felt that Bibi ought to be getting fresh food, raw or freshly cooked; a greater variety; and much more interesting texture and taste than the little jars could provide, marvellous emergency standby though I found them.

I am a fanatic reader, too, of all the small print on the wrappers of manufactured foods, which tells you exactly what is in them, in descending order of quantity. Some of the contents surprised me. Why on earth add sugar to a savoury dish like spaghetti? And others seemed to consist of surprisingly high proportions of low-value starchy foods – wheatflour, barley and so on. We can do better than that for Bibi, I thought.

But just what, exactly, do you cook for a baby? None of my own generation seemed to know much about it. I also found that although there are thousands of lovely cookery books for grown-ups on the market, covering every conceivable aspect of eating, there was not at that time a single one for babies.

And I felt appallingly ignorant. I didn't know what a baby needs, how much, or how often. I didn't know which foods you can give a baby, and which you should not. I didn't even know at what stage a baby stops merely ingesting pap and starts chewing. I didn't know much.

So, rather belatedly, I set about giving myself a crash course in nutrition, and in no time at all became a perfect bore on the subject, earnestly expounding on vitamins and protein to my friends. The kitchen filled up with wholewheat flour and jars of wheatgerm; white bread and biscuits were banished in disgrace; and the milkman noted a daily order for yogurt.

I found an enormous colourful chart which showed the principal sources of vitamins, proteins, fats, carbohydrates and minerals, and why your body needs them. It was hung in a prominent place on the kitchen wall, and Ineke and I, with many thoughtful glances at it, set about working out a series of dishes for Bibi that would take no more than a few minutes of preparation and cooking.

I pored over cookery books and nutrition tomes, experimented at weekends and in the evenings, adapted my favourite grown-up recipes, and picked the brains of all my girl-friends with babies. And on weekdays I typed sheets of experimental recipes for Ineke to try out. Every morning she would set to work on them with chopping board or grater, mouli, grinder, blender or mincer, often simplifying or modifying them. From time to time we conferred. If a recipe turned out to be wonderfully simple and a big hit with Bibi, it went into a growing collection in a big navy folder on the kitchen shelf. If it took hours of fiddling and used up every cooking implement in the place, we threw it out ruthlessly – whether Bibi liked it or not.

Some of our most masterly dishes were resounding flops. We thought them perfectly delicious, but after one mouthful Bibi's mouth stayed firmly closed. (At a later stage it simply opened up so that the food came tumbling out again.) My husband once watched, fascinated, while I tried out a new liver recipe on seven-month old Bibi: liver wrapped in foil with a little butter, onions and herbs, baked in the oven then mashed with broccoli.

'Bibi's face,' he wrote, 'was a study. Polite as always, she opened her mouth, took a bite, closed her eyes to open them again, first in bewilderment, then in anguish, and at last in deep disgust. She swallowed carefully and opened her mouth for the second bit, and the third . . . and the fourth. It was all too obvious that the liver was, to say the least, not her favourite dish . . .'

Some of the most childishly simple dishes we worked out, on the other hand, thrown together in desperation when the cupboard was a bit bare or time a trifle short, were the greatest of hits with Bibi: huge grins, cries of delight, sighs of disappointment when her plate was empty. Courgettes, for instance: cleaned, sliced and steamed for a couple of minutes until tender, then served with a great dollop of cream cheese and fresh herbs from my window-box: that was one of Bibi's greatest favourites.

As she grew older, I grew bolder and more confident. At nine months Bibi was the youngest person I have ever known to reek of garlic. She took to fish, adored yogurt, chewed happily on fresh fruit, even lemons – and very occasionally, even ate up her liver like a good girl. I was relieved to note, too, that home-cooking seemed to be doing her nothing but good: she slept like a top, had far more energy than she knew what to do with, never knew the meaning of colic, constipation or diarrhoea – and the worst illness she suffered from was a feverish cold.

All the dishes we tried out successfully were written down by me, together with a note of the time they took to prepare – and Bibi's reaction: enthusiastic, indifferent or just plain disgusted. The pick of the collection is printed here, together with others worked out since when our second daughter, Ninka, arrived. I hope they will save lots of other hardworking, first-time-around mothers some of the anxiety, the research and the hours of time experimenting that they cost me. I have included, incidentally, some of the dishes that Bibi didn't fancy a bit. Babies, like grown-ups, have their own decided tastes in eating, and other babies might fall on the same dish with happy cries.

Some of the recipes take only minutes to prepare and cook. Others take little preparation, but need time in a slow oven – good for days when it is on anyway for the family's Sunday lunch, or when you are making a casser-ole for the evening.

I make absolutely no apology, finally, for the extreme simplicity of some of the recipes. The most leisured mother in the world, after all, doesn't want to fiddle about all morning producing six ounces of mini-lunch.

1

Mother v. Specialist

Let us face facts: home-cooking for your baby IS rather more trouble than opening up another little tin or jar; and not even – at least until you get the hang of it – all that much of an economy.

But what it should never be is the appalling anxiety that so many new mothers seem to have been brainwashed into finding it: an endless nutritional obstacle-course studded with snares and pitfalls, and their baby the loser every time they make a mistake. The babyfood companies play delicately on these insecurities in their advertising and promotional literature. 'Every mother needs to know that the food her baby eats is every bit as wholesome and nutritious as the food she prepares for the rest of the family,' says one. 'We make certain that our meals contain protein, vitamins and minerals your growing baby needs,' runs another. '. . . taken with breast or baby milk, they'll provide a nutritionally well-balanced diet.' 'Working with an eminent nutritionist (who is an expert in the dietary needs of babies and growing children) we have developed – after painstaking research and testing – a selection of baby meals which . . . contain only pure and wholesome ingredients,' boasts yet another.

The way they all go on, you'd think that feeding a small baby was a job so complicated and so specialized that the average mother would be insane to think of tackling it.

It's not just the worrying chat about protein and vita-mins and minerals that's calculated to make mothers feel so inadequate. It's the sheer giddy variety of the menus: Liver and Bacon, Golden Chicken Dinner, Vegetables and Turkey, Braised Steak Dinner, Pineapple and Cream Dessert, Mixed Fruit Pudding ... 'At mealtimes the menu seems endless. Up to seventy-five delicious varieties' one advertisement used to run, filling me with gloom.

Now in many ways the babyfood companies do an admirable job, and make a creditable effort to keep up with new findings in infant nutrition. Most – if not all – of them now conscientiously avoid chemical colouring, flavouring, preservatives. At least one of them actually advises its customers not to start babies on solid foods before four months, which is pretty noble of them, considering. There's an excellent new range of wholesome Mixed Vegetables with added protein and Vitamin D for vegetarians, or for mothers who don't want to feed too much meat to their babies. One or two of them show distinct signs of trying to play down or phase out the added sugar which so many of their customers demand. The foodstuffs the babyfood companies use are, they assure us, meticulously chosen, and carefully and hygienically prepared.

And for sheer convenience, of course, commercial babyfoods are unbeatable in a crisis: Bank Holidays, unexpected guests, travelling, Christmas, sudden illness in the family – at times like these there's certainly a place in any mother's life for instant babyfood. And very welcome it will be, too.

But you don't need to be all that much of a nutritional wizard to realize that however conscientiously the babyfood companies carry out their brief, the nutrition they offer a baby is still far from ideal.

Fresh vegetables lightly cooked, ripe raw fruit, easily digested protein like mashed yolk of egg, chicken or cottage cheese, health-building foods like yogurt and wholewheat cereal – that's the diet a small baby thrives on. If, though, she's fed exclusively out of tins and jars, she'll be living largely on precooked pap, padded out with high-calorie fillers like rice-starch and wheatflour.

For your baby's tea, for instance, you could mash up half a ripe banana, stir in a teaspoonful of yogurt, add a squeeze of fresh orange juice. For around 8–10p, you're giving your baby the clean, delicious taste of raw fresh fruit with all its vitamins and minerals intact, plus the healthy B vitamins, protein and calcium in yogurt.

Alternatively, you could spend 22p on a jar of Banana Yogurt Dessert. Then your baby will be getting Water, Low Fat Yogurt, Bananas, Sugar, Modified Cornflour, Maize Oil, Vitamin C – in that order. Sugar is discussed in the next chapter; chemically modified cornflour has little nutritional value, and if you want your baby to develop a sweet tooth – feed her little puddings which taste as yuckily sweet as this.

Don't feel, either, that your baby is hard done by unless she gets a dazzlingly different little pud every day. The only taste she's been used to up to now, remember, is milk: even one new taste is going to seem like a big adventure.

And certainly don't be pressured by clever advertising into feeling that if you do decide to give your baby fresh food, you'll spend the next few months fretting over a hot stove to produce a thousand mini-meals. One lightly-steamed green vegetable mashed up with a little cottage cheese is a staggering blow-out for a six-month-old baby, and perfectly adequate nutritionally. No meal, at this early stage, need be much more complicated than that, and if you look at p.112, you'll see a whole week's menus for a six-month-old baby, of dishes involving little more than five minutes' cooking or preparation at a time.

By the time your baby is ready for something a little more adventurous, you'll be feeling much more confident yourself, and ready to tackle something slightly more ambitious; and you'll be an expert by the time she's a toddler. There's another week's menus for this stage on p. 113.

It's difficult to work out much more than the approximate economics of home-cooking for a baby because so much of the food she eats will be in your house for family meals already: apart from yogurt and cottage cheese, there may be very little you buy specially. Estimating the cost of a diet of commercial babyfood is even trickier, because prices, brands and sizes – not to mention a baby's appetite – all vary so enormously.

But I was curious to know the answer, all the same. So I conscientiously listed all the ingredients of my two weeks' menus, shopped for them at the most competitive local supermarkets, and did my best to calculate costs and portions. On the same day, I shopped for the commercial babyfoods too. I allowed for a child with an average appetite, for a tin or jar sometimes to do double duty, took advantage of special offers on what certainly aren't in my view the best brands, and bought the two weeks' supply from the cheapest local source.

Verdict: feeding your baby out of tins and jars all the time couldn't cost you much less than £5.26 a week, whereas a diet of fresh home-cooked food shouldn't come to more than £3.08 at the outside.

By the time your baby is a toddler with a healthy

growing appetite, it will be even cheaper to cook for her yourself. A diet consisting entirely of bought babyfood – though I'm sure no mother nowadays would think of such a diet for her toddler – couldn't cost much less than £6.63 weekly, whereas fresh raw or home-cooked food should come to approximately £4.52.

Neither menu, incidentally, includes the milk and the fresh fruit juice which are likely to be on your baby's daily menu, nor have I included them in my costings, since they'll be the same in both cases.

As you can see, home-cooking wins hands down in terms of economy too

2

Who Needs A Bouncing Baby?

Until recently, it was generally taken for granted that as long as a baby's weight rose steadily, week after week, ounce by gratifying ounce, the child was doing fine: the fatter the fitter, only of course nobody spoke of 'fat' babies – they were 'chubby' or 'bouncing'.

It is now known that babies – in this as in so many other respects – are no different from adults. Feed them a well-balanced diet supplying all the proteins, fats, vitamins and minerals they need, and they will grow steadily and enjoy splendid health. Stuff them with sweets, starches, and junk food, on the other hand, and you will make them fat just the way an adult becomes fat on such a diet. With one sinister difference. The fat adult presumably has some idea of what he is doing to himself. In the case of babies, you could well be landing the poor things with a weight problem which is of your making, but which they will have to battle with for the rest of their lives. They will become junior members of a very large club: while millions in the Third World starve to death, other millions in the rich countries of the West are compulsive over-eaters, with an obesity problem which can be a real threat to health as well as a lifelong sentence to painful dieting. And worrying numbers of these fat people are babies and small children.

It's not just the weight problem that is important. Overfed and poorly fed children are seldom happy or healthy. And you don't need to take my word for it:

there's an easy, fascinating way to check this truth with your own eyes. Again and again I have found that I had only to glance at the mothers with babies and small children in my local supermarket to guess at once what they had filled their trolley with. The bright-eyed, active, healthy-looking children were riding happily along behind loads of fresh fruit and vegetables, cheese, eggs, yogurt, wholemeal bread. Spot an overweight, tired-looking woman dragging a puffy-faced, fretful-looking, over-weight child with her, on the other hand, and you can bet any odds you fancy that the trolley will be loaded with biscuits, sugary cereals, packet desserts, frozen sweet mousses and ice-creams, tinned puddings, tarts, bottled fizzy drinks, sausage rolls, cakes and meat pies, with no fresh fruit or vegetables worth speaking of. The most extreme case I ever remarked was a cross-looking woman dragging a spotty-faced, snotty-nosed, whining child with her: her shopping basket was filled with tins of canned spaghetti, packets of chocolate digestives – and many cans of 'Hi-Protein dog food Enriched with Vitamins and Minerals'. (Presumably the dog at least was bright-eyed and healthy.)

How do you know which foods are fattening for your baby? Easy: just look at your own diet sheet. All the things you have been brainwashed into laying off – excess fat and sugar in particular – are precisely what you ought to be cutting out of your baby's diet, or feeding her in carefully controlled quantities.

When I was a diffident new mother wondering what to give Bibi next, there was still a widespread belief that sugar was, somehow, a Good Thing, and that babies and small children were badly deprived if they didn't get it.

We now know that far from being a Good Thing, sugar

is highly undesirable in anybody's diet, especially that of a small baby – and I'm speaking now of the refined stuff that turns up in powder or syrup form, rather than the sugars naturally found in fruit and milk.

Health experts today agree that babies – like adults – don't need sugar, and are much better off without it. And if you can save your baby from developing a sweet tooth for life by keeping her off sugar in infancy, surely it's irresponsible even to let her taste the stuff as long as you're boss. Manufacturers of baby foods pay lip service to this truth: 'sweet foods can cause overweight and tooth decay, and a child's first teeth are just as important as his adult teeth', says a helpful little booklet issued by the makers of Robinson's Baby Foods, which young mothers can pick up at their Baby Clinic. Most baby food manufacturers today have stopped adding sugar in any form to savoury items like Spaghetti Bolognese – a quite common practice when Bibi was a baby. Robinson's themselves make an attractive range of baby juices such as Apple and Peach with no added sugar. And Mothercare's new range of baby foods 'made entirely from pure, wholesome ingredients. . . .' are advertised as containing 'no added sugar (sucrose) or salt'.

But we live in the hard world of commerce, and baby food manufacturers cannot afford to be too far ahead of their customers. 'Our policy is to use the minimum sugar necessary to produce an acceptable flavour', as one of them diplomatically phrased it to me. For 'acceptable' read 'heavily sweetened', and I'm told on good authority that if those little baby desserts don't taste sweet, thousands of mothers will probably shovel a couple of spoonfuls of extra sugar into them. Which is probably why some of Mothercare's sucrose-free baby puddings turn out to contain, instead, dextrose and or honey, both members of the happy sugar family. The taste isn't as sweet, and the quantities are quite small, but most dental experts agree that dextrose (otherwise known as glucose) and honey are still bad news for teeth, even if not as lethal as sucrose.'A rose by any other name – all good tooth-robbing stuff', comments Richard Cook, the dentist whose book 'Sugar Off!' published by Great Ouse Press, may open your eyes to what sugar can do to your baby's budding teeth.

So presumably it's the relentless pressure of public demand that produces those horrific brightly coloured baby fruit syrups which loudly proclaim the extra vitamin C they contain to build firm teeth and gums, while in fact they're loaded with glucose or sucrose to help rot those first teeth in their gums – not to mention the artificial colouring, flavouring and preservatives that some of them contain, chemical additives which have no place in a baby's diet. Incredibly, too, all but one of the teething rusks on the market also contain sugar, though the makers of one brazenly label it the New Low-Sugar Rusk.

And although Heinz have successfully launched a range of Pure Fruit 'with no added sugar', most of those teensy little puddings in tins and jars are gourmet concoctions rich in all the goodies that as adults we have learned to avoid: how about Cream Caramel Dessert, for instance, made with Skimmed Milk, Caramelized Sugar, Cream, Modified Cornflour, Flour, Sunflower Oil, Glucose Syrup?

We British have, of course, the sweetest national tooth in the Western World. We also have incomparably the worst teeth. To me it is tragic and appalling that a five-year-old should have even one cavity in her teeth. But the Court Report on Child Health, published in 1976, turned up the horrifying fact that in a huge sample of average five-year-olds, less than a third had perfect teeth – and nearly a third had at least five teeth which had begun to decay. And almost 40% of people in this country have lost all their natural teeth.

It nice to be able to report that the 1980s have seen an encouraging downturn in the figures. But as a nation we keep an unbelievable number of confectionery businesses in operation (just count the sweet shops and kiosks next time you walk down your local High Street); our national best-selling soup is a sweetish tomato soup; our favourite vegetable is the ultra-sweet green pea; we love to eat sugary pickles and jammy ketchups even with meat. And when we want to give pleasure to a small child – we offer her sweets.

The plain, unvarnished truth about sugar is that in nutritional terms it gives nobody anything but calories: in other words, fat. As John Yudkin wrote to *The Times* on 23 March 1973: 'Sugar really can claim to be the "purest" of all our foods . . . Guaranteed free from trace elements, vitamins or any other nutrient . . . it is a substance for which the body has absolutely no physiological need.'

Many mothers, I suspect, add sugar to their baby's cereal, drinks and puddings, not only because it has been suggested to them that the baby 'needs' it, but because they simply can't imagine enjoying them without sugar themselves. Luckily, this isn't true if the baby hasn't already acquired a sweet tooth from too much sugar. Bibi, for instance, cheerfully ate up her cereal with milk and grated fresh fruit but no sugar, as a baby. Today, a lovely twelve-year old, she and her sister Ninka start their day with sugarless and sometimes quite sharp freshly pressed orange juice, like plain yogurt, as well as sweetened fruit ones, love cubes of cucumber and carrot as a snack, and eat masses of fresh fruit, skin and all. We have taught them to be proud of their strong, healthy teeth, and dinned it into them that sweet-eating or gum-chewing will ruin them. We never have cakes or sweet biscuits in the house except as extra-special treats. Pocket money is rarely spent on sweets. And although both children will make a grab for the stickiest, gooiest, creamiest looking cake in sight at a party, they usually abandon it after a mouthful or two.

My own conviction, in fact, is that babies have excellent natural palates, and can appreciate a wide range of flavours. If they are fed from the word go on bland and sweetened pap, however, then that is probably what they will grow up liking best.

3

Diet for a Well-balanced Baby

Millions of mothers the world over cheerfully bring up their children without ever having heard the daunting words Protein, Carbohydrate, Vitamin, Mineral or Balanced Diet. They use their common sense and their instinct. And there's certainly no need for you to go to night-classes in nutrition – another of those intimidating words. All you need is enough basic information to take the worry out of it. So here it is.

Basically, what you dish up for your baby's next meal will fall into one of five categories: Milk; Other Dairy Products and fats; Eggs, Fish and Meat; Fruit and Vegetables; Cereals. So before we start juggling them around to produce that famous 'balanced diet', let us take a closer look at them.

1 MILK: In a class of its own for babies: and the healthiest, happiest babies are breast-fed. Permanently on tap, guaranteed sterile, always exactly the right temperature, and specially designed for mini-digestive systems, breast-food is the perfect balanced food for a baby. Breast-fed babies certainly suffer less from the colics, the odd stomach upsets and the digestive problems which can be such a worry to new mothers. They're protected, too, against other infections, since their mother's own antibodies are passed to them through her milk. And there's growing evidence that much of today's crop of allergic disease – hay fever, migraine, eczema and asthma among

them – can be triggered by a too-early introduction to cow's milk and other foods, before a baby's digestion is mature enough to cope with them. More and more hospitals today encourage mothers to breast-feed; and even if you gave up the idea initially and resorted to bottle-feeding, it's often possible to re-establish breast-feeding, given enough help and encouragement from a trained breast-feeding counsellor. (See pages 118–19 for useful Addresses.)

Breast-milk or one of the baby-milk formulas are complete foods for a baby, and during at least the first four or five months of her life, she should need nothing else. And for at least the first year of her life, it's likely to be her most important food. Milk is marvellous stuff. It contains protein – the basic raw material from which healthy babies are constructed. It's rich in calcium, which builds bones and teeth. It contains some iron – vital for good healthy blood – and fat for energy. It contains Vitamin A – essential for resistance to infection and general health; some of the B vitamins; a little Vitamin C; and some vital minerals. It has one more great charm for a busy mother, once her baby is turning into a toddler and past the weaning stage: it is still Instant Food, needing no preparation whatever.

2 OTHER DAIRY PRODUCTS AND FATS: cheese, butter, yogurt, vegetable oils.

Cheese is fattier than milk, but otherwise, it has most of the same nutritional bonuses – protein, calcium, Vitamin A. And although lots of people may suggest to you – as they did to me – that cheese is somehow 'wrong' for a baby, don't listen to them – they're talking through their hats. Grated cheese stirred into lightly cooked green vegetables or scrambled eggs (I found a mild cheddar best); cream cheese piled in dollops on top of steamed green vegetables; slices of very soft cheese as a tea-time treat or between meals; cheese made into a sauce for gratiné dishes – these are just some of the ways babies will take to cheese. (Forget about using it as a topping under the grill, though – it goes so tacky and rubbery that tiny jaws cannot cope.) Don't forget cottage cheese, either: Bibi ate it by the spoonful when it was interestingly flavoured with chives; and when it is plain, you can add it to stewed or fresh fruit just like cream.

Yogurt contains lots of the useful things in milk like calcium and protein, although in smaller quantities. But it has one speciality of its own: the bug Acidophilus, which sets up a sort of do-it-yourself production-line of B vitamins inside you, and keeps your stomach and gut functioning easily and sweetly. Babies fed plenty of yogurt seldom know what an upset stomach is, which is lovely for their mothers. Bibi ate masses of it, mainly the plain kind, whipped up or blended with grated fresh fruit, or stirred into cereal. Incidentally, don't get agitated when you see the magic word 'live' on pricey health-food-shop yogurt. All yogurt is live unless it is so sour that you would not want to eat it. And if all your family loves it, you can save money by producing quantities of it at home: see my recipe on page 110.

Butter, and *Pure Vegetable Oils*, supply some of the fats babies need in their diets to keep skin and nerves flourishing. But don't overdo these fats, obviously: other foods like milk, cheese and egg yolk also supply them.

3 EGGS, MEAT AND FISH: all good sources of the complete protein that babies need for growth. There's a

vague general belief that meat supplies a *better* kind of protein, but fortunately for vegetarians this is untrue: the protein in eggs and fish is just as good, yogurt and cottage cheese are two other excellent sources of complete protein, and any of these are easier on a baby's still immature digestive system than meat. So there's no point in rushing it onto the menu, and no reason to feel that your baby is deprived until she's tasted real beef steak.

What would mothers do without eggs, I often used to ask myself, thankfully popping one into a pan of water for Bibi's tea. No fuss, no mess, the perfect convenience food, six whole grammes of first class protein, and plenty of other nutritional pluses: Vitamins A, D and B, for instance, and iron – possibly the first taste of this vital mineral your baby will ever have is a spoonful of well-cooked egg yolk. Some babies are allergic to the whites of egg, although they usually grow out of this eventually; and by the time your baby is a year old, she can be eating a whole egg at a time: scrambled with cheese, or tomato, or with shreds of ham and kidney stirred into it; or baked in a cocotte with a spot of butter and fresh herbs; or soft-boiled; or poached – or about fifty-seven other ways.

Lean Meat is a first-class source of the protein babies need for growth; and as long as it's in a manageable form – stewed, minced, mashed or puréed – almost any lean meat is good for babies, although pork is too rich for them, and bacon is low on protein. (If meat is too tough and tacky to purée properly, it's too tough for a baby anyway.) Chicken is especially lovely for babies, as well as being about the cheapest meat around: it can be minced into manageable form with a fork quite often. Most butchers – and many supermarkets – sell minced veal as well as minced beef and don't mind a bit, I found, serving you minute baby-sized amounts of it; so don't be shy of asking for as little as three ounces.

Liver has a terrific bonus: it contains all the B vitamins, which help keep babies good-tempered little persons and excellent sleepers, as well as just plain healthy. Unluckily, liver is one of the hardest of all foods to make palatable for tiny children: I experimented with several recipes before I found one that Bibi will almost always eat up with enjoyment (see Baked Liver and Onion, p. 84).

Fish for a baby? Well yes, why not? But lots of people mysteriously think it's an odd idea, and advise you darkly against it. I suppose it's part of the national prejudice against fish in any form other than coated in batter and deep-fried. The fact is, however, that fish is excellent food for babies and small children, and has lots of protein and plenty of iron, iodine and useful trace elements in it besides, as long as you are careful not to overcook it. Bibi ate fish and loved it from the age of seven months. I must admit, though, that I used to go through and through it with agonized concentration and a small fork, because I was so terrified of seeing her choke on a fish bone; and in that respect, perhaps, it is less attractive to nervous new mothers than other forms of protein. However, if you stick to cod-steaks and the occasional fillet of plaice, you shouldn't need to worry; and those small frozen bricks of boneless cod are a godsend to baby menus.

4 FRUIT AND VEGETABLES: are vital to your child's health because of the vitamins and minerals they contain. I personally think it is important to get her used to the interesting savoury taste of vegetables like carrots, onions and spinach just as fast as she gets to enjoy chewing an orange or eating bits of delicious apple. But

for mothers with babies who are fussy or difficult about eating up their nice spinach, it can be a huge relief to know that in terms of food values, fresh fruit and vegetables are virtually interchangeable, and as long as your baby is getting one or the other, it doesn't much matter which, at this stage. Fruit is more fattening because it contains so much sugar, that's all. Fresh orange juice, bananas, lightly stewed apple, pears or peaches are all fruits you can safely feed babies from five or six months, together with almost any vegetables except the most exotic, as long as the texture is right. There's no need to cook fruit as long as it's soft and completely ripe.

Remember that the skin is, nutritionally, the best part of most fruit and vegetables – and then remind yourself to wash both carefully, in case they may have lingering traces of pesticide or fertilizer clinging to them.

And for babies – as indeed for gourmets – the faster and more lightly you cook vegetables, the better. Most of their goodness and all of their delicious flavour is preserved when you steam them, covered, over boiling water until they're just done. When they are stewed to a soggy mess, their goodness goes down the drain with the water. So does any pleasure in eating them – as most boarding-school pupils or hospital patients could confirm.

5 CEREALS: bread, flour, all the breakfast cereals supply carbohydrates for body heat and energy – calories, in other words. When they are unrefined wholegrain cereals complete with the germ and outer husk or bran, they also supply invaluable vitamins, especially B complex and E, iron, calcium, magnesium, zinc and other important trace elements, together with the fibre needed for a healthy gut. Most of these goodies disappear when flour is

refined. It was once thought cranky to insist on wholemeal bread instead of white: not any more. Modern nutritional science has shown that refined carbohydrates like white flour and sugar can cause many of the health problems which plague the affluent West – with heart disease high on the list. But health reasons apart, I have always been an unabashed fanatic about wholegrains on the grounds of taste and texture. How anyone can prefer that flabby white sliced stuff to a lovely nutty wholemeal loaf baffles me – and I notice that the wholemeal has always vanished from the shelves of my local supermarket long before the white, so presumably more and more housewives feel the same way. I use wholemeal flour for almost all cooking, too, and I keep a stock of wheatgerm – the richest part of the wheat grain – to enrich breakfast cereals, or add to the topping of gratiné dishes and fruit crumbles. (You can buy plain wheatgerm in packets quite cheaply; Bemax and Froment are commercial names for the same thing. Once opened, it should be kept in a screw-top jar in the fridge, or it may go rancid.)

There are various breakfast cereals for babies on the market, but many of them are to be avoided because they contain sugar, while others are mixtures of refined carbohydrates like white rice and wheatflour which lack the nutritious goodness of whole cereals. Many experts think, too, that cereals shouldn't be added to a baby's diet too early, and that since wheat-allergy is so common, it might be better to start with other cereals. So you could give your baby muesli – perfectly easy to make at home if you have a blender-grinder, much cheaper than the bought kinds, and much better. Or you could give her whole rice: wash it carefully, add enough water to cover it generously, seal up the saucepan or casserole, and either cook it on a very low flame, or in a fairly slow oven, for about 50 minutes to an hour. Stir in a little yogurt: it's nice served cold, too.

So that's what will be going on the menu. How do you balance it so that it's a varied, healthy diet for your baby?

For the first few weeks of mixed feeding, that's hardly a problem: milk is still her staple diet, and eating at this stage is as much for educational purposes as for actual nutrition: a nibble of this, a spoonful of that; as long as it is not all fattening cereal, you can hardly go wrong.

But by the time a baby is six or seven months old, you need to plan the menu a little more thoughtfully. Your baby still needs her milk, first and foremost. She needs protein: an egg, a little chicken, a little steamed fish, a spoonful of plain yogurt or cottage cheese. She needs the fats supplied by butter or pure vegetable oil, the B vitamins in yogurt or wheatgerm, and the vitamin A in cheese, though she doesn't need all of them every day. She needs the vital Vitamin C and minerals in fresh fruit and vegetables: not just endless orange juice, but whatever ripe delicious fruit is in season – peaches, plums, bananas, or strawberries if they do not upset her stomach (they do some babies). Vegetables can supply a little bulk to a meal as well; potatoes, carrots and swedes are lighter and less fattening than rice or bread. Finally, babies need some cereal in their diet. But they don't need anything like the quantities some mothers pile into their luckless babies: once a day is quite enough. Nor will they object if the cereal is not sweetened, though it might taste horrible to you.

If you're still worrying yourself silly over how much of this or that your baby ought to be getting, turn to the sample menus on pp. 112–13 to look for a few ideas. And do remember that unless a baby's palate and feeding instincts have been wrecked by excessive amounts of bland, sweetened pap, they have a perfect natural instinct – like a healthy little animal – for what is good for them. They will never starve themselves, nor gorge themselves sick. So if they make it plain that they'd love another helping of mashed bananas and orange juice, give it to them. And if they push away their cereal after one spoonful, don't try force-feeding tactics: they've had enough, thank you, and as much as is good for them.

4

So What's Wrong With Shellfish?

From time to time, the brand-new nervous mother, casting around among her family, friends and advisers for ideas – any ideas – on what to feed her baby, comes up against mysterious taboos.

Some of these are totally unfounded – as in the case of fish, for instance, or cheese. Nor could I ever find a convincing reason why Bibi shouldn't be allowed onions in her diet when she was six months old, so I gaily gave her onions – and, indeed, garlic from time to time – with no perceptible ill effect, although they might upset other tiny stomachs.

But other foods are on the Not-Advisable list for excellent reasons. Pork is too rich and indigestible for small stomachs. And I also steer clear of preserved meats like sausages, corned beef and luncheon meat: the sodium nitrate used to preserve them is beginning to worry nutritional experts even for grown-up stomachs, so why take a chance with your baby?

Some babies are allergic to egg-white: start with the yolk only at first, and don't overcook it till it is unattractively dry.

All forms of shellfish – though loaded with protein, and rich in iron and iodine – are out just in case your baby might turn out to be allergic to them, which would be very nasty for you both.

Mushrooms are too rich and indigestible, and cabbage, sprouts and cauliflower may be a bit windy – babies don't care much for the pronounced flavour, as a rule. Before you feed tomatoes to a baby, incidentally, remove the skin and pips.

Strawberries sometimes upset babies, and unripe fruit should always be avoided. So should sugar, other than the natural sugar – lactose or fructose – found in milk, fruit and vegetables. Better to give your baby fresh strained orange juice to supply her Vitamin C than those sugary highly-coloured syrups you can buy at the chemist, however much enriched with Vitamin C they may be. And most rusks on the market are both sweetened and relatively pricey: a stick of carrot or apple, or fingers of wholewheat bread, baked hard, are much better all round for teething gums to chew on.

For children of any age, finally, I avoid like the plague all processed, packaged food commercially prepared with too many additives in the form of flavouring, colouring, stabilizers, etc. One widely sold and highly popular packet pudding on the market, for instance, lists as its ingredients the following: sugar, starch, sodium phosphate, edible vegetable oil with antioxidant, permitted emulsifiers, lactose, sodium caseinate, flavourings, whey powder, lecithin, colour. Nutritional junk, in other words, almost useless to your child's health apart from the milk which the instructions tell you to add – and which you pay extra for anyway. I'd sooner give Bibi a piece of cheese and an apple for her tea.

Too many mothers, I suspect, have a sneaking feeling that, somehow, puddings are 'right' for their children, and that they are neglecting their maternal duty if they aren't cooking up some sweet little mess for junior's tea. If you find yourself yielding to this persuasion, take a grip of yourself, and another look at your diet-sheet.

5

The Allergy Headache

When Bibi was a baby, nobody bothered much about allergies. Today, it's yet another worry for brand-new mothers. But it's important to keep the possibility in mind – especially if there's a history of hay-fever, asthma, eczema or migraine on either side of the family – because you could save your child – and yourself – an awful lot of problems both now and in later life if you're sensible about it.

If both you and your husband enjoy rude health, and if you're planning to breast-feed your baby until she's six months old or more, probably you don't need to give the matter much thought. Susceptibility to allergy tends to be passed on from parent to child, and most of the evidence strongly suggests that breast-feeding for as long as possible gives babies the best protection against such problems. (Breast-fed babies have been known, though, to react to something their mother ate: shellfish, for instance, or lots of garlic: so if you're breast-feeding your baby and she develops a digestive upset after her feed, think back to the last meal or two and try to work out what caused it, so that you can avoid it for the time being.)

Go carefully when you introduce her to solid foods. Her digestive system was, after all, programmed to cope with mother's milk for at least the first months of her life: even the most cunningly devised baby formula could be a bit of a strain, and bombarding her with solid food when she's barely three months old could be asking for trouble.

Allergy – sensitivity to certain foods or drinks – can manifest itself in any number of ways, and many doctors still shy away from the whole notion of allergies. But repeated bouts of colic, wind, diarrhoea and foul-smelling motions are all strong suggestions that trouble is brewing down in the digestive tract, while other less obvious danger signals should be watched for, if they keep happening: excessive dribbling, a runny nose, perspiration, eczema, persistent sleeplessness, stuffy nose and chronic ear infections.

'The later you introduce solid foods, the better', advises immunologist Dr David Freed. 'Four months should be about the earliest – six months is better still. Mothers shouldn't be pressured into starting on solids until the baby is ready – and let the baby give the lead. Weaning should be very gradual: breast-feeding should be tailed off slowly. A breast-fed baby has been exposed to small doses of whatever its mother eats, even before birth. So it seems to me that the first solid foods it eats should be those its mother also eats, suitably mashed up of course. By the same token, though, mother would be well advised not to be lashing into the dairy products and wheat too often during pregnancy, and while she's breast-feeding. A good healthy nourishing diet, well varied, with nothing to excess, is the best way to avoid trouble.'

The two foods most likely to cause problems are indeed milk (which means butter and cheese too) and wheat. (But there are plenty of others – so don't let it get you down.) Other foods to which susceptibilities are very common include shellfish, strawberries and pork, none of which you're likely to feed to a six-month-old baby anyway. It would be sensible, accordingly, to go easy on these at first, and start with simple little purées of ripe pear, banana, carrots or potatoes. Mash them up with a little breast-milk or yogurt, which is less likely to cause problems than milk. Don't start her on straight cow's milk until she's at least six months old. And when you first give milk, cereal or indeed any new food, let a few days go by before you try it again, to see if any problems show up. Starting her on a non-stop diet of cereals is asking for trouble.

And if you have any worries at all about your baby's diet, consult your doctor. If he seems unreceptive to the possibility that it could be an allergy problem, insist on a second opinion, or write to one of the addresses I've given on p. 119.

How Not to Bug Your Baby

Almost everyone knows that you wash your hands after going to the loo, that kitchens ought to be clean, and that sneezes spread germs. Apart from these basic factors, however, I suspect that most of us are woefully ignorant on the subject of hygiene in the kitchen. I know I was. I also know that I found it amazingly difficult to discover exactly what is and what is not safe practice in home catering. So I make no apologies for setting out the elementary rules here.

Rule One: If you cook more than you intend to serve that day, cover the rest of it and put it into the fridge or larder at once. Slowly cooling food is heaven for bugs to breed in.

Rule Two: So is warmed-up yesterday's food, unless it is heated right the way through: half the mystery-bug outbreaks in schools and hospitals are probably due to those depressing lukewarm slices of joint roasted hours back. When you are reheating yesterday's cooking for baby's lunch today, make sure you reheat it gently to boiling point: that will settle the bugs.

Rule Three: Even when you have stored it immediately in the fridge, don't keep cooked baby-food hanging about for more than a day; in other words, two lunches, starting with today's, is the maximum you should make at one go.

(*Three* identical lunches in a row begins to seem like a case for Baby's Lib, anyway.)

So now you know.

7

Blenders, Mincers and All That

Cooking for babies doesn't call for a lot of specialized and costly kitchen equipment. At a pinch you could manage perfectly well with ordinary kitchen pots and pans, plus the help of a friendly local butcher prepared to put small quantities of meat through the finest blades of his mincer for you. Mothers happily prepared baby-foods for centuries before blenders and mincers were invented, after all.

But cooking for a baby is, all the same, a splendid excuse for adding to your kitchen a small number of gadgets, pots and pans that you'll go on finding useful long after your baby has grown into a strapping schoolchild. Here's my list of those that could be specially useful:

1 A BLENDER: The baby-cook's best friend. You can use your blender to purée all sorts of grown-up food into suitable mushiness for very small babies. Do remember, though, that a fast light touch is essential for successful blending: food with absolutely no texture at all is boring even for babies. You can make instant baby dishes from whatever suitable ingredients happen to be available. Blend together, for instance, a slice of very lightly sautéed liver, a couple of small boiled potatoes, a couple of lettuce leaves or sprigs of parsley, and milk, stock or water to give it all a creamy consistency. (Remember when whipping up Instant Baby Lunch that blenders need a good bit of liquid to work well.) Using your blender, too, you can whip up delicious creamy, frothy fruit drinks which no small child

can resist – especially if she was watching open-mouthed when you whizzed it. Try, for instance, a couple of stewed apricots in their juice, a few flakes of almond, a pinch of freshly grated nutmeg, and a cup of milk. Or a glass of orange juice, a spurt of lemon juice, and a couple of tablespoons of yogurt. To plump a drink out and make it creamier, add yogurt; to make it sharper and more interesting, a dash of lemon juice. And if your child is looking pale and peaky, and needs building up, a big blender drink is a low trick for slipping heaps of goodness into her with no grief at all. Chop a banana into your blender, add a big spoonful of yogurt, a small spoonful of dried brewers' yeast, and a glass of milk: whizz it, and that's at least half the nourishment your small child needs in a day, and a completely adequate meal in itself, rich in calcium, magnesium and the B vitamins. (I often make it for myself, for extra winter energy.) You can buy blender-grinders for as little as £15 – the Moulinex ones are incomparably the best value, in my view. Kenwood, on the other hand, do a special half-litre baby-sized one, which would always be useful for sauces, or for just one portion of soup. The grinder part of your blender will be equally useful – to make your own baby-muesli, for instance. New on the market are electrically operated hand-blenders, very versatile since you can use them in pan or jug or bowl without having to transfer the contents into a special container.

2   A HAND-OPERATED SIEVE: and there's nothing on the market to touch the French-made *mouli-légumes*, once more by Moulinex, a jolly orange plastic job with three different gauges of sieve. I've been using one for years to purée my thick vegetable soups, and it does a

marvellous job on baby-foods too, tackling anything but the stringiest of meat without reducing it to boring glutinous pulp. If you can't afford a blender, you could certainly get by with a *mouli-légumes*. Better still, Moulinex now make one specially for baby-food: the *Mouli-Baby*, selling for under £3. Creamy vegetable soups – the kind that are so solid they're almost a meal in themselves, and a standard teatime treat for lucky French babies – come out less tiresomely bland from a Mouli than from an electric blender.

3   A FOOD PROCESSOR: the luxury that turns into a necessity almost as soon as you own one. Everybody who has a food processor will tell you that they can't imagine how they ever managed without it, and having owned a Magimix for six months, I see exactly what they mean. It will chop, grate, mince, purée, slice, all in the twinkling of an eye. With its help, baby can join the family Sunday lunch: slice off a bit of lean meat from the joint, drop it in with some of the vegetables (though not, please, the rich roast potatoes), and two seconds later, there you are, instant baby-food. Steamed cod or haddock minced with a small potato and a couple of peas, spinach puréed with a spoonful of yogurt, fresh carrots shredded to a pulp so fine you can cook them in minutes, potatoes sliced paper thin – these are some of the dishes that will invent themselves once you get the hang of a food processor.

4   A STEAMER: steaming is a fast, clean way to cook food, conserving most of the natural juices of fish or vegetables, along with their vital nutrients. If you don't have one of the old-fashioned steam-pans with a perforated bottom that will sit on top of another pan, you can

buy, for under £3, a collapsible, sectioned stainless steel steamer on tiny little feet, that will sit inside another saucepan and expand from small to capacious so that it will fit almost any size saucepan – which makes sense if you're steaming a single tiny potato or a lonely sprig of broccoli.

5   A SMALL LIDDED CASSEROLE: baby lunch tends to get a bit lost in that family-sized casserole. So I bought Bibi her very own traditional brown earthenware one, the half-pint size, and I cooked enough lunch in it for two meals when she was eight months old, and for one when she was eighteen months old.

6   SMALL-SIZED WHITE CHINA RAMEKIN: comes in useful for baking fruit, for egg-custards or rice-puddings. But one of my girl-friends with a freezer simply uses the small-sized foil dishes as a substitute for both baby casserole and small china oven dish: she says they do perfectly well.

7   A COUPLE OF SMALL-LIDDED POLYTHENE OR GLASS CONTAINERS for storing tomorrow's supply of lunch in the fridge.

8   A SMALL SAUCEPAN: fairly solid and preferably non-stick, for cooking all the top-of-the-stove dishes – always useful later on for milk or sauces.

8

The First Blow-out: When?

As bewildered first-time mothers soon discover, nothing changes faster than fashions in baby-care. We are only just emerging from an era when it was considered that babies could hardly start on solid foods too soon, and new mothers boasted to you about the amount of cereal their tiny baby was guzzling daily.

I remember a friend of mine telling me proudly that her three-month-old son was already on three square meals a day. 'He had orange juice and cereal for breakfast,' she related, 'turkey and pineapple for lunch, and chocolate pudding for tea.' (A diet, incidentally, that I couldn't contemplate myself without nausea, but that's by the way.) Is this a record? Absolutely not. A survey on infant sleeping patterns, some years ago, turned up the incidental information that some of the babies involved had been put on solid foods at the age of a mere two weeks.

Sanity is slowly returning. Even the baby-food companies now suggest to their customers, in accordance with official thinking, that four months is quite soon enough to start even bottle-fed babies on mixed feeding, unless your doctor specifically recommends an earlier start. And for breast-fed babies, six months is usually quite soon enough – a blissful economy of time, energy and cash.

Quite apart from the extra expense and work of mixed feeding, too early a start certainly isn't a good thing for a baby nutritionally. On the contrary. Before going on to solids, your baby will probably be drinking up to two pints of breast or bottle milk a day. Two pints of milk contains as much body-building protein as a king-sized steak, or half a dozen eggs, or one of those big cartons of cottage cheese. So you can see that your little daughter would have to be eating like a little piggy to get even half the protein she needs from solid food, though it slips into her so effortlessly in the form of milk. And no amount of steak or eggs could supply the bone-building calcium she needs – of which milk, once more, is such a lavish source.

So why the mad rush? There are only two good reasons for shoving either milk or solid food into a baby. One is to satisfy her raging appetite so that she lets up crying. The other is to nourish her so that she grows and stays healthy. She has all the rest of her life to learn to eat like a civilized person instead of sucking at breast or bottle. And if she falls asleep after one feed, and sleeps peacefully until it's time for the next one, if she doesn't always even finish her bottle, you needn't be in any special hurry to get her eating as well as drinking.

If, however, she's already crying for her feed long before time, if she's still acting hungry when it's all over, if she's already drinking pints and pints of milk a day – then by all means try giving her solid food, after she has drunk her milk.

Try her with little nibbles of this and that in a small, soft plastic spoon from time to time: mashed hard-boiled egg yolk, lightly steamed green vegetables, yogurt, ripe banana, home-made thick, creamy soup (the kind that's almost solid – for which there are lots of recipes further on), cottage cheese or mashed carrots. If she's very much at the experimental stage, and nothing much is getting eaten, give it a rest and try again a little later. But always give her breast or bottle first, and go on to solid food afterwards only if she is hungry enough and curious enough to have a go.

You are probably giving her vitamins A and D in the form of drops. And if she is still on a formula milk, it almost certainly contains iron, Vitamin C and some of the B vitamins. If not, mashed hard-boiled egg, puréed liver or spinach for iron; yogurt for the B vitamins; and freshly pressed, strained orange juice for Vitamin C are the first extras you might consider.

After that it's up to you – and your baby's appetite.

9

The Non-Eating Baby

You've planned, you've shopped, you've spent a not inconsiderable amount of time preparing a delicious lunch for your baby. You tie on her bib, sit her down, and set it in front of her. And what happens?

She pushes it away untasted. Or she uses her spoon to flip it all over the floor in one swift movement. Or she closes her eyes and clenches her mouth and waits for it to go away. Or she sobs heartbrokenly at the mere sight of it. Or . . . well, anyway, you can see she's not going to eat it.

This could be for one of several reasons:

(a) She's on strike because it's liver again and she can't stand the stuff.
(b) She's decided to play you up and this looks like a great moment.
(c) She's off-colour.
(d) She just doesn't happen to be hungry at the moment, thank you very much.

If it's (a) it's only kind to give her something else – like one of your emergency store of little jars, which she will wolf down with provoking demonstrations of appreciation and enjoyment.

If it's (b) play it by ear, but resign yourself beforehand to another load of wasted cooking effort.

It's almost never (c) but if it is, you will know anyway.

And if it's (d) there is absolutely nothing you can do about it except not worry. Babies have a very strongly developed sense of self-preservation, and I have yet to hear of one starving itself to death.

Meantime, what of that wasted lunch?

If you're an optimist, you could always cover it up and stick it in the fridge and present it again at the next meal-time.

If you're a realist, though, you'll steel yourself.

Chuck the whole lot into the dustbin and remind yourself of the immortal words of I forget whom: 'It doesn't matter if babies don't eat so long as the mothers don't finish it up for them and get fat.'

10

A Note on Seasoning

You don't miss what you've never had; and the milk off which babies live for the first months of their little lives is neither sweetened nor salted. Keep their solid food that way too, for the first months. Medical research has made us aware of the perils of both salt and sugar in a baby's diet, so I have eliminated both from the recipes in this book, leaving it up to you to decide at what age you want to start adding a little seasoning to your child's food. You may find, incidentally – as I did when I retested all the savoury recipes without salt – that the flavour of fresh vegetables cooked with no seasoning at all comes as a startling revelation.

To make a change from time to time, stir in a spot of cheese, or fresh or dried herbs. And when you boil or steam vegetables, don't throw the water away; save it to use as a vegetable stock in a baby casserole or soup (you did remember not to salt it, didn't you?); it will give delicious extra flavour, not to mention all those precious vitamins and minerals that so often get washed away down the kitchen sink.

11

How To Use the Recipes

In each of the five sections of recipes that follow, you will find, first, a group of recipes marked with a single star (*), and planned for five- or six-month-old babies just starting on solid foods. Then there are more recipes, marked with two stars (**), for older babies who have developed enough bite and appetite to appreciate something a little more adventurous.

The one-star recipes, for absolute beginners, are ultra-simple and extremely easy to prepare: purées of vegetables with or without fish or meat, cheese or egg; fruit; cereal. The quantities suggested will produce one handsome blow-out for the beginner – probably more than she can cope with most of the time. But resist the temptation to save the rest for another try later; warmed-up, mushed-up carrots aren't much encouragement for a beginner, and a certain amount of waste is unavoidable at this stage.

By the time your baby has been slogging away at her purées and cereal mushes for two or three months, she will be quite used to eating, and learning to chew or even bite with her gums, whether or not she can boast a single tooth. It's now time to ease off the blending and start giving her food with more texture and chewiness to it; what the baby-food companies usually call Junior Food, packaged in the next-size-up jars.

At this stage, you can either go on giving her the simple one-star recipes, only mashing them roughly with a fork instead of blending them or putting them through a wider mesh of your *mouli-légumes*. You may find, too, that you need to increase the quantities slightly. Or else you can now move on to the two-star recipes. These recipes are still extremely simple to prepare, often with no more than four or five ingredients. But they are all dishes that are quite attractive and appetizing enough for a grown-up to eat as well – I still use several for family Sunday lunch. And if you are going to the trouble of cooking for your baby, you might just as well make some for yourself too, instead of the hurried cold snack to which busy mothers so often resort. So the two-star recipes are all designed in quantities big enough to make a meal for mother as well as baby; if you're cooking for a toddler too, just top up the ingredients all round. Don't forget, though, to add the salt and pepper your grown-up palate craves, after you have extracted the baby's portion.

Most of the two-star recipes shouldn't present a problem for a baby who has already learnt to chew. If in doubt, just rush a baby portion through your *mouli-légumes* before dishing up.

12
Super Soups

*Carrot and Potato Soup

½ medium carrot
1 medium potato
150 ml (¼ pint) chicken broth or vegetable stock
1 small raw tomato

Wash and scrape carrot, wash potato. Cut both into tiny cubes to reduce cooking time. Add to the broth, bring to the boil, simmer until the vegetables are soft – about 10 minutes – put everything in the blender, add the tomato, skinned, de-seeded and chopped. Blend.

*Lentil Soup

1 tablespoon dried lentils
1 medium carrot
a little chopped onion or garlic
150 ml (¼ pint) chicken broth

Pick over the lentils then soak them overnight. Wash, scrape and dice carrot, chop onion finely, put lentils, carrot, onion or garlic, and broth into a small pan, bring to the boil. Simmer till the vegetables are soft – about 15 minutes. Blend.

*Fish Soup

1 medium carrot
½ medium potato
a little chopped onion
a small chunk of white fish – coley will do very well
150 ml (¼ pint) milk
butter
parsley or chives

Wash and scrape the carrot, wash the potato, cut both into tiny cubes for fast cooking. Put the potato, the carrot, and the finely-chopped onion into a small pan with the fish, cover with the milk, add a little nut of butter. Simmer gently till the fish is cooked – about 3 minutes. Take it out, leaving the vegetables to simmer. Skin the fish, flake it, doublecheck for bones. When the vegetables are soft put them and the fish in the blender, add the milk they have been cooked in, and blend. A little parsley, or a few chives added to the blender makes it prettier as well as tastier.

*Turnip and Potato Soup

½ small turnip
1 small potato
150 ml (¼ pint) milk
sprig of parsley

Thinly pare and dice the turnip, wash and dice the potato, put both in the pan with the milk, bring to a gentle boil, and simmer till the vegetables are soft – about 10 minutes. Put in blender with parsley – add a dash more milk if necessary. Blend.

Fresh Pea Soup

450 g (1 lb) fresh young peas
2 spring onions
2½ cups vegetable stock or water
milk
sprig of mint

Shell the peas and chop the spring onions. Put them into a small saucepan with the mint. Add the stock or water and cook gently till the vegetables are tender – about 15 minutes. Pass the soup through a fine *mouli*, or blend, and add enough milk to give a creamy consistency. Reheat but do not boil.

A blob of yogurt floating on top is fun.

Cauliflower and Tomato Soup

½ small cauliflower
225 g (½ lb) tomatoes
300 ml (½ pint) chicken or vegetable stock
basil – fresh or dried

Wash the cauliflower and cut into small pieces. Peel, de-seed and chop the tomatoes. Put the vegetables into a heavy saucepan. Add stock and basil. Bring to the boil, cover and cook gently until the cauliflower is tender – about 10 minutes. Allow to cool slightly and then put through a blender. Reheat and serve.

Blender Carrot and Orange Soup

225 g (½ lb) small carrots – or 3 medium ones
300 ml (½ pint) milk

¼ teaspoon dill weed
juice of 1 orange
parsley

Scrape the carrots and chop into thin rounds. Put them in a pan with the milk, add the dill weed, bring to a gentle boil, then cover and simmer till the carrots are just tender. Let the cooked carrots and milk cool slightly then put them in the blender and blend for a second or two. Add the orange juice, blend for 2 minutes. Reheat, stir in some finely chopped parsley and serve.

Tomato Soup

1 medium onion
4 or 5 tomatoes
1 large potato
butter
1½ cups milk or vegetable stock
basil – fresh or dried

Peel and chop the onion, slice the tomatoes in half, wash and dice the potato. Melt a big knob of butter in a pan, add the chopped onion, and let it cook gently. Put in the tomatoes on top, leave them till their juices run, then add the milk or stock, the potato pieces and the basil. Bring to the boil, simmer gently till the vegetables are tender. Then fish out the tomato skins, and put the rest through the finest sieve of the *mouli*.

**Carrot Soup

225 g (½ lb) young carrots
1 onion
1 very small turnip
butter
stock or milk and water
fresh herbs – parsley, marjoram or mint

Scrape and slice the carrots, peel and finely chop the onion, and peel and chop the turnip. Melt a big knob of butter in the pan, lower the heat, add the carrots, onion and turnip, and let them cook gently in the butter for about 15 minutes, taking care that they do not turn brown. Add a big cupful of stock if you have it, or half milk and half water. Bring to the boil, add the fresh herbs, then cover and simmer for about 45 minutes. Add a little more milk if necessary, and sprinkle with chopped parsley.

**Leek and Potato Soup

2 fat leeks
2 large potatoes
large knob of butter
600 ml (1 pint) stock or water
a little watercress
fresh parsley or mint
milk

Cut off the white part of the leeks, clean them thoroughly and slice them. Wash and chop the potatoes. Melt the butter in a heavy saucepan, add the leeks, turning the heat right down, and let them cook very gently in the butter – do not let them colour or you'll ruin the delicate creamy flavour of this soup. Add water or stock, potatoes, watercress and herbs. Bring to the boil, cover and simmer gently till the potatoes have softened. Blend or put through the *mouli* and add enough milk to make it creamy.

**Winter Soup

2 onions
2 potatoes
2 carrots
butter
2 cups stock or water
parsley
milk

Peel and chop the onions. Wash and slice the potatoes. Scrape and slice the carrots. Melt a knob of butter in a pan, add the onions and cook them gently. Add the stock or water, put in the carrots, potatoes and fresh parsley. Bring to the boil, then lower the heat, cover and simmer until the vegetables are tender – about 30 minutes. Put through a *mouli*, reheat and add enough milk to give it a creamy consistency.

13
Fish Dishes

At today's prices, fish is hardly a Best Buy for baby's luncheon, and few mothers nowadays would even consider buying it just to make tiny-sized meals. So most of the recipes in this section are for two-star dishes, for mother and toddler to share. I have included a small number of one-star dishes, for occasions when a fish meal is being made for the whole family, and there is a spoonful or so of cod or hake to spare.

*Spanish Cod

small chunk of cod or coley
1 new potato
milk and water
1 small tomato
sprig of parsley

Put the fish in a small pan with the scrubbed potato and enough milk and water (half and half) to cover it. Bring to the boil, simmer gently till fish is tender – about 3 minutes: take out the fish, leaving the potato to cook. Skin the cod, remove any bones: skin, de-seed and chop the tomato. When the potato is cooked, peel off any remaining skin, chop it and put it with the fish and the chopped tomato in the blender. Add the parsley, and enough of the milk-and-water mixture to turn it into a creamy consistency. Blend.

*Fish and Cheese Dinner

1 small piece of coley
½ small onion
150 ml (¼ pint) milk
parsley
1 small carrot
about 1 teaspoon grated cheese

Chop the onion finely, put it into a small pan with the milk and parsley, bring almost to the boil, add the fish and turn the heat down. Simmer for 2 or 3 minutes till the fish is cooked, remove it to another dish, and add the scraped and grated carrot to the fishy milk. Leave it to simmer while you flake the fish and scan it for hidden bones. Then put the fish in the blender. When the onions and carrot are soft, add them to the fish, with the grated cheese, and pour in enough of the fishy milk to make a smooth creamy purée. Blend, reheat, and serve.

*Special Salmon

Because of its price, salmon is *always* special these days – even in tins. But if you have a scrap left over from a family feast of fresh salmon, here is a cold summer dish a baby might love.

Cold cooked salmon
a chunk of cucumber
yogurt
chives or parsley

Check the salmon for skin and bones, then flake it. Pare the cucumber and if the seeds are too big, remove them.

Then chop it, and drop it in the blender. Add the flaked fish, and a tablespoon of fresh yogurt, together with a few chives or a sprig of parsley. Blend.

*Fish Cream

    small chunk of cod, haddock, or coley
    butter
    ½ small onion
    wholewheat flour
    a little milk

Melt the butter in a small pan. Finely chop the onion and add it: let it cook gently over a low heat. When it is golden but not coloured, sprinkle a coffeespoon of flour over it, stir. Add enough warmed milk to make a creamy sauce – about 2 tablespoons – stir again, and let it cook very gently for about 5–10 minutes. Meanwhile, skin the fish, if necessary, and check for bones; then add it to the onion sauce and cook for another 3–4 minutes, or until the fish is tender. Mash it all together, doublechecking for tiny bones.

*Fish Stew

    small piece of boneless white fish
    spoonful of mixed diced vegetables from a stew-pack
    milk and water
    butter
    parsley

Take a spoonful of diced frozen vegetables from one of those stew-packs that most supermarkets sell: put them in a pan, cover with half milk and half water, bring to the boil, simmer till all the vegetables are tender. Take them out and keep warm. Put the piece of fish in the milk-and-water mixture, let it simmer for 4 or 5 minutes till cooked. Meanwhile, mash the vegetables, adding a spot of butter. When the fish is tender, add it to the vegetables. Blend, adding a sprig of parsley, and a little of the milk and water from the vegetables.

*Scrambled Roe

1 dessertspoon soft roes
butter
1 egg
a little milk

Melt a knob of butter in a small pan, add the roe and let it soften. Beat the egg, beat in the roe together with a small spoonful of milk, then scramble it all gently in the same buttery juices. Serve with crustless fingers of wholemeal bread.

**Haddock Cream

170 g (6 oz) haddock
300 ml (½ pint) milk
butter
1 rounded dessertspoon flour
3 tablespoons frozen peas
a little grated onion

Poach the haddock for 5 minutes in the milk. Melt a knob of butter in a saucepan, stir in the flour. Gradually add a

cup of the hot fishy milk to make a creamy sauce. Stir in
the frozen peas, grate in a little onion, and cook over
gentle heat for about 10 minutes. Stir in the flaked
haddock and let it all heat through gently.

**Tuna Mash

   3 tablespoons tinned tuna
   5 or 6 new or 2 medium potatoes
   milk
   a little grated onion
   butter
   wheatgerm

Wash and thinly slice the potatoes into a small pan. Cover
with milk, grate in a little onion. Bring to the boil, lower
the heat and cook gently until the potatoes are done and
the milk almost all absorbed. Mash the potatoes with a
fork, stirring in a small knob of butter, and stir in the tuna,
from which you have carefully removed oddments of skin
and bone. Turn into a small buttered casserole, sprinkle a
little wheatgerm over the top, dot with butter and brown
under a hot grill.

**Fish Pudding

   piece of smoked haddock
   1 large cup milk
   fresh herbs – mint or parsley
   slice of lemon peel
   2 medium potatoes
   wheatgerm

Put the milk into a small pan, add fresh herbs, the lemon peel, and bring to the boil. Lower the heat, slice the potatoes thinly, and add the fish and potatoes to the milk. After 3 or 4 minutes, the fish will be cooked. Take it out – leave the potato cooking – skin it, doublecheck for bones, and flake it into a small buttered casserole. When the potato is cooked, mash it with a fork in the fishy milk and put it on top of the fish in the casserole, sprinkle wheatgerm over the top, dot with butter, and brown under a grill for about 5 minutes.

Haddock with Onion and Tomatoes

170 g (6 oz) haddock
butter
a small slice of onion
2 large tomatoes
milk

Melt a knob of butter in a pan, grate the onion into it, and let it cook gently for a minute. Put in the skinned and boned haddock, together with the skinned and chopped tomatoes and a couple of tablespoons of milk. Bring to the boil, lower the heat, and let it all cook very gently together for about 10 minutes, turning the haddock over gently once or twice. Mash it all together with a fork, turn into a dish and serve.

Grilled Herring Roes

Herring roes (the tinned kind do very well for this)
oil

wheatgerm
butter
lemon juice
fresh herbs – parsley or mint

Brush the roes with a little oil, and sprinkle them with wheatgerm. Put the roes on a piece of oiled foil-paper and under a red-hot grill for about 10 minutes. Do not turn them. Melt a little butter, squeeze in a little fresh lemon juice, add some chopped parsley or mint, and pour it over the roes. Serve with plain boiled potatoes, or brown bread and butter.

**Grilled Fish and Cheese

170 g (6 oz) cod or other firm white fish
wheatgerm
butter
2 dessertspoons grated cheese

Pat the fish dry, and sprinkle with a little wheatgerm. Heat the grill, and melt a knob of butter on a piece of foil in the grill pan. Put the fish on this buttery paper, turn it over almost immediately and grill for a few minutes until it is tender and cooked through. Remove all the bones from the fish, flake it into a dish, add the grated cheese and mash through with a fork.

**Cod in Cheese Sauce

170 g (6 oz) cod steak or other firm white fish
25 g (1 oz) butter
1 rounded dessertspoon flour

300 ml (½ pt) milk
2 tablespoons grated cheese

Skin the fish, remove all bones, and chop it in small pieces. Make a sauce by melting the butter in a pan, stirring in the flour, and then adding the warmed milk little by little till you have a thinnish creamy sauce. Stir in the fish and cook for another 10 minutes over a very gentle heat. Then stir in the grated cheese and serve at once.
NB. Frozen fish is fine for this dish.

**Baked Fish Custard*

170 g (6 oz) haddock fillets
2 courgettes
butter
lemon juice
1 egg
¾ cup warm milk
nutmeg
¼ teaspoon dill weed
wheatgerm

Preheat the oven to 190°C (375°F), gas mark 5. Wash and slice the courgettes. Skin and slice fish into very small pieces. Feel each piece with your fingers for bones – even if it's supposed to be filleted! This is the only safe way of checking. Butter a shallow heatproof dish and lay the fish in it. Sprinkle with a little lemon juice. Blanch the courgettes in boiling water, then drain them and pat dry with paper. Put them on top of the fish. Beat the egg in a bowl, add the warm milk, stir in the nutmeg and dill weed, then pour the mixture over the fish and courgettes. Sprinkle with wheatgerm. Put the dish in a small roasting tin filled with cold water. Bake in the oven for 45 minutes, or until the custard is set and browning nicely on top.

14

Meaty Meals

Being served the same dinner four times running is enough to put any baby off mixed feeding: and throwing away untasted three-quarters of a lovingly-prepared Baby Beef Dinner is enough to put any mother off home-cooking for her child. The fact is that a baby consumes such tiny quantities of meat at a sitting that it's almost never going to make sense to buy and cook meat *just* for her dinner, while she is still an absolute beginner.

Instead, plan her meat meals round the family menu. If you're having a roast for Sunday lunch, cut a tiny slice of lean meat for baby, and purée it with some of the vegetables. If you are all eating stew or casserole in the evening, make it early in the day – reheated stews are always nicer anyway – with a minimum of seasoning, and purée some of it for her lunch; then season it to the family's taste, and reheat it for your dinner. Cold lamb, minced and served with a fresh purée of cucumber and tomato, is lovely summer food for a baby; in winter, cold roast beef minced and gently reheated in a little stock, then stirred into a creamy purée of winter vegetables, swedes and turnips, carrots, spinach or potato. Chicken, finally, is not only the softest and most digestible of meats, and ideal for a small baby on this account but it is also the cheapest, and likeliest to be figuring on the family menu: so most of the one-star recipes at the beginning are for simple chicken dishes.

Lamb and Courgette

> 1 small slice of cold, roast, lean lamb
> a little stock
> 1 small courgette

Mince or *mouli* the lamb, put the warmed stock in a small pan, and heat through thoroughly. Meanwhile, scrape and chop the courgette into chunks, steam until tender – a couple of minutes – then mash. When the lamb is hot, stir into the courgette purée. Blend if necessary.

Braised Liver

> 1 small piece of liver
> a small slice of onion
> butter
> water

Chop the onion very finely. Melt small knob of butter in a small pan and gently fry the onion in it. Add the liver cut up into small pieces and a dessertspoon of water. Let it braise gently until cooked through, then chop or *mouli* the liver and onions together. Serve on its own, or stirred into mashed potato or spinach.

Chicken, Yogurt and Cucumber Purée

> 1 small piece of cold chicken, skinned
> chunk of cucumber
> 1 dessertspoon yogurt
> chives

Cut the cold chicken in small pieces, pare and chop the cucumber, removing the largest seeds. Put chicken and cucumber in the blender with the yogurt and chives. Blend. Very refreshing for a hot summer day.

Chicken and Tomato I (Summer version)

  1 chunk of cold cooked chicken
  1 medium tomato
  1 teaspoon plain cottage cheese
  1 sprig parsley

Skin, de-seed and chop the tomato. Skin the chicken. Put chicken, tomato and cottage cheese in the blender, with the parsley to make it look pretty. Blend. Another hot-weather treat.

Chicken and Tomato II (Winter version)

  piece of cold cooked chicken, skinned
  a little stock
  1 medium tomato
  a slice of onion
  a sprig of parsley

Mince the chicken, stir in the stock which you have heated gently in a small pan, and heat for 10 minutes. Skin, chop and de-seed the tomato, add to the chicken, put in the blender with the remaining ingredients and purée. Reheat gently and serve.

*Steak Special

For occasions when there is some tasty steak in the house: save a very small slice of it for baby's lunch.

    steak
    1 small new potato
    a little milk
    1 small slice of onion
    butter

Steam the potato, skin and mash with a little milk. While the potato is steaming, butter a piece of foil, heat the grill to red-hot. Finely chop the onion, and put it on the buttered foil under the grill. When the onions are soft, add the piece of steak, and grill it for a couple of minutes on either side. Mince or grind the steak and onion with its buttery juices and add to the mashed potato.

*Chicken Liver Treat

When you make the Poached Chicken on p. 87 for the family, add the giblets to the water in which the chicken is cooked but save the liver till the chicken and vegetables are almost cooked. Then add it and let it simmer in the rich stock for about 15 minutes. Take a spoonful of potato, a little of the carrot and leek, and the liver: mash them all together.

**Greased Lightning Casserole

    225 g (8 oz) minced beef or lamb
    1 small onion

1 slice green pepper
1 large potato
thyme – fresh or dried
3 tablespoons stock or water

Chop the onion, finely slice the green pepper, chop and
dice half the potato. Mix these all in with the minced
meat, seasoning with a little thyme. Put them in a lightly
oiled casserole, cover with the rest of the potato, thinly
sliced, spoon over the stock, if you have it, or water, cover
tightly, and bake for about 1 hour in a moderate oven,
180°C (350°F), gas mark 4.

NB: This is a favourite standby for Sundays and other
hectic days. It can be made almost in seconds, makes no
washing-up other than a chopping-board and knife, and
cooks at whatever speed you want – 30 minutes in a hot
oven if you are in a rush, or over an hour in a slow oven
while the family goes for its Sunday morning walk.

**Mince Casserole

225 g (8 oz) minced beef
1 small onion
oil
1 small garlic clove
2 large tomatoes
basil – dried or fresh
thyme or parsley
2 tablespoons stock or water

Chop the onion and cook gently in a little oil heated in a
casserole. Add the minced meat mixed up with the

chopped garlic and the finely-chopped tomatoes. Season with a little dried basil (fresh is even nicer) and a little thyme or parsley. Add the stock or water, cover tightly, and bake in a moderate oven, 180°C (350°F), gas mark 4, for about 1 hour.

**Meaty Soup

If you have made one of the thick, tasty soups in the first section, and want to make it into a meaty winter-time dinner – just add meat: a piece of steak lightly oiled, grilled lightly under a red-hot grill; the little nut of meat in a lamb cutlet; a piece of cold cooked chicken, a chunk of braised steak from a stew. Just *mouli* or mince them, stir them into one of the thick soups – Leek and Potato Soup, Carrot, Tomato or Winter Soup, for instance – and let them heat through gently.

**Courgette Casserole

    225 g (8 oz) minced beef or lamb
    4 courgettes
    butter
    1 small onion
    basil – fresh or dried
    grated cheese
    ½ cup stock

Clean and thinly slice the courgettes. Butter a small casserole and line it with some of the slices. Finally chop the onion, mix it with the minced meat, season with a little basil, and put into the casserole. Top with another layer of courgette slices and cover with grated cheese. Bake in a moderate oven, 180°C (350°F), gas mark 4, for about 1 hour.

NB: This was the greatest success ever with Bibi. Abandoning our usual one, two, or three-star rating system, we gave it *six* stars, three exclamation marks, and the word 'fantastic' heavily underlined . . .

**Veal Casserole

    225 g (8 oz) lean veal
    butter
    2 medium carrots
    1 small onion
    1 potato
    basil – fresh or dried
    1 cup stock or water

Preheat the oven to 170°C (325°F), gas mark 3. Heat the grill to red-hot. Sear the veal for 3 or 4 minutes, turning it so that all sides are lightly grilled. Put it in a lightly oiled casserole. Grate in the carrot; add the onion, finely chopped. Clean, chop and add the potato. Season with a little basil. Add enough stock or cold water just to cover. Cover. Put in the oven and bake for 1½ hours.

NB: Beware of bargain-priced pie-veal when shopping for this dish. It can sometimes be very tough and rubbery.

**Veal Pie

    225 g (8 oz) minced veal
    butter

1 small onion
1 small green pepper
basil or freshly chopped parsley
4 small courgettes
stock, if you have it

Lightly butter a small casserole. Finely chop the onion and the green pepper, mix with the veal, add a little basil or freshly chopped parsley. Put into the casserole. Clean and finely slice the courgettes and cover the veal with them. Dot with butter, pour over a coffeecup of stock, if you have it: the water in which the vegetables have been cooked, or plain water, will do. Cover with foil and a lid. Bake in a moderate oven, 180°C (350°F), gas mark 4, for 45 minutes.

Bibi's Irish Stew

3 lamb chops or 340 g (¾ lb) stewing lamb
2 small onions
2 medium potatoes
thyme
5 tablespoons stock

Trim the fat off the chops if you are using them; if using stewing lamb, trim off most of the spare fat. Thinly slice the onions, wash and slice the potatoes fairly thickly. Put the meat at the bottom of a saucepan, cover with the chopped onions, top with a thick layer of potatoes. Season with a little thyme – fresh or dried. Pour over stock, bring gently to the boil, turn the heat right down. Cover the pan tightly and leave to cook for at least 1½ hours, when the onions and potatoes will have melted into a savoury mush, and the meat will be tender. Pick the meat off the bones, and mash it into the vegetables with a fork.

Lamb Stew

225 g (½ lb) stewing lamb
wheatgerm
fresh or dried thyme
vegetable oil
1 small potato
2 small carrots
1 small turnip
1 small onion
a few peas
water

Sprinkle the pieces of lamb with wheatgerm and thyme. Heat the oil in a frying-pan and fry the lamb very quickly, turning it so that it is slightly browned on all sides. Put the pieces in a saucepan, add the potato, carrots, turnips and onion all cleaned and chopped, and the peas if you have them. Put in enough water to cover and bring to the boil. Cover the pan, turn the heat down until the stew is gently bubbling, and simmer until the meat is tender – up to 1½ hours. Take out the pieces of lamb, pick off the tender bits of lean meat, discarding the bone and bits of gristle. Put the meat in a dish with the vegetables and juices and mash all together.

NB: Watch out like a hawk for the odd tiny sharp bone that tends to lurk in lamb.

Lamb and Apple

  2 lamb chops
  1 crisp apple (Granny Smith or Bramley)
  lemon juice
  fresh thyme

For this recipe, you need a small flameproof casserole which can sit easily under a grill. Heat the grill. Trim the fat off the chops. Wash and finely dice the apple and put it in the dish. Sprinkle with a little lemon juice, season with the thyme. Put the chops on top, grill for 7 minutes, turn them over and grill on the other side for another 7 minutes. Take the meat off the bone, mash it with the apple using a fork. For small babies, mince.

Kidney Casserole

  1 veal or lamb kidney
  1 carrot
  1 small onion
  1 potato
  butter and oil
  a few peas if you have them
  marjoram – fresh or dried
  water

Preheat the oven to 180°C (350°F), gas mark 4. Clean and chop the carrot, the onion and the potato. Clean and trim the kidney, leaving it whole. Heat a little butter and oil over a high flame, put in the kidney and quickly sear it on all sides. Now slice it, discarding the bits of fat and put it in a casserole, together with the onion, potato, carrot and peas. Season with a little marjoram. Add a coffeecup of water, cover tightly, and cook in the oven for about 1 hour.

**Steamed Liver

170 g (6 oz) calf's or lamb's liver
1 small onion
2 or 3 small carrots
2 or 3 small potatoes

Wash and slice the onion into large slices. Scrape and slice the carrots. Wash the potatoes. Steam them all together until almost tender – about 20 minutes – and then add the liver and steam for a few minutes more. For small babies, mince or *mouli* it all together. For toddlers, *mouli* the liver only, mash the vegetables, season with a little chopped parsley, add the liver.

**Liver Casserole

170 g (6 oz) calf's or lamb's liver
oil
2 carrots
1 small onion
2 small potatoes
1 cup stock

Brush the slices of liver with a little oil. Heat the grill to red-hot and sear the liver, turning it over once. Then put the liver in a small casserole. Finely slice the carrots, chop up the onion and put them both in with the liver. Slice the potatoes thinly and put on top. Add the stock, cover tightly, and bake at 140°C (275°F), gas mark 1 for 1 hour.

NB: Liver is very much more tender when grilled first in this way.

**Baked Liver and Onion

    170 g (6 oz) lamb's liver
    2 rashers of bacon
    wholewheat flour
    fresh or dried thyme
    oil
    1 onion
    water

Preheat the oven to 180°C (350°F), gas mark 4. Thinly slice the liver and roll the pieces in wholewheat flour seasoned with a little thyme. Heat the oil in a frying-pan and sear the liver lightly on both sides. Then put the liver in a lightly-greased casserole and sprinkle with the finely chopped onion. Lay the rashers of bacon on top, add a coffeecup of water, cover with foil or its own lid and bake in the oven for about 40 minutes.

**Chicken with Rice

    1 large leg or wing of chicken
    1 small onion
    butter
    fresh herbs – mint or parsley
    2 tablespoons milk

300 ml (½ pint) water
2 tablespoons brown long-grain rice

Peel and finely chop the onion and skin the piece of chicken. Melt a small knob of butter in a pan, put in the chopped onion and turn it about until it is soft and golden. Add the chicken, and the fresh herbs. Put in the milk and enough cold water to just cover, add the rice and simmer gently for 30 minutes, or until the chicken is tender. Take out the chicken, and simmer for another 10 minutes or until the rice is cooked. While the rice is cooking, take the chicken meat off the bones and shred into a dish with a fork. Add the rice when it is done.

**Spanish Chicken

1 large leg or wing of chicken
2 large tomatoes
1 onion
oil
3 tablespoons water
fresh herbs – mint, parsley or basil

Skin the piece of chicken. Skin the tomatoes (it helps to drop them in boiling water for a few seconds first). Peel and chop the onion. Heat a little oil in a small pan, put in the chicken and brown it lightly. Add the onion and the chopped tomatoes. Add the water and some chopped fresh herbs – mint, parsley or basil. Bring to the boil, turn down the heat, then cover and simmer gently for about 30 minutes. Transfer the tomatoes and onions to a small dish, take the chicken off the bone and mash it in with the vegetables.

NB: In Spain, where the chickens are tender and delicious, this was a standby and a great favourite of Bibi's. Since Spanish garlic is milder and sweeter than the kind you buy in this country, I usually added a little, chopped, to the dish.

**Chicken and Carrot Cream*

  1 large leg or wing of chicken
  1 medium carrot
  2 teaspoons chopped onion
  parsley
  ½ cup chicken stock
  2 dessertspoons yogurt
  grated cheese

Chop the carrot and put in a small saucepan with the chicken, chopped onion and parsley. Add the stock, bring to the boil, cover and cook over a gentle heat for 25 minutes. Extract the chicken piece from the stock, remove the skin, pick the meat off the bone and chop it into lumps. Put the carrots and 2 tablespoons of the cooled stock into the blender. Blend for a second or two, then drop in the chicken lumps one at a time, add the yogurt and blend again. Pile into two buttered cocotte dishes, sprinkle tops with grated cheese and heat through in a hot oven, 200°C (400°F), gas mark 6, for about 10 minutes – or 25 minutes if refrigerated first.

**Poached Chicken

    1 chicken
    the whites of 2 leeks
    1 large onion
    2 large potatoes
    2 carrots
    butter
    oil
    fresh herbs
    water

Wash and slice the leeks, peel the onion and chop finely, wash the potatoes, and scrape and slice the carrots. In a large pan melt a big knob of butter, add a little oil, heat it and brown the chicken a little on all sides. Tip out the butter – probably a bit burnt by this time – add 300 ml (½ pint) of water and put in all the vegetables except the potatoes, together with the fresh herbs. Bring to the boil, lower the heat, then cover and simmer very gently – the liquid just bubbling – for 45 minutes or until the chicken is tender. Add the potatoes after the first 20 minutes.

NB: Strictly speaking, this is a family dish which I cook when I want lovely poached chicken for lunch – with plenty left over to eat cold later on with mayonnaise, or to use for chicken risotto with rice. The stock makes the basis of a delicious soup. For baby meals, just carve off a small piece of chicken and blend it with some of the vegetables. And if you buy your chicken from an honest butcher or supermarket who supplies the giblets with it, see the recipe for Chicken Liver Treat on p. 76.

**White Rabbit

   2 140 g (5 oz) pieces of rabbit
   25 g (1 oz) butter
   1 dessertspoon wholewheat flour
   300 ml (½ pint) milk
   a dash of allspice
   1 large potato
   A teaspoon grated onion

Wipe rabbit pieces with kitchen paper, put them in a pan of cold water, bring briskly to the boil, remove any scum which may come to the surface, then reduce heat and continue simmering for 5 minutes. Melt butter in a small saucepan, stir in the flour, add the heated milk. Season with a dash of allspice, stir and leave to cook on a gentle heat for a few minutes. Remove rabbit from the water. Wipe dry and place in a medium heatproof casserole. Pour over the sauce. Bring to the boil, cover and cook in a medium oven, 180°C (350°F), gas mark 4, for about 1 hour. During the last 20 minutes add the thinly-sliced potato. Shred the rabbit with a fork, removing any bones. Mash potatoes in the sauce, add the meat. Serve with a green vegetable. Any sauce left over makes a good soup for supper.

**Chicken Rehash

   cold cooked chicken
   butter
   1 dessertspoon wholewheat flour
   chicken stock (if you have it)

coffeecup milk, warmed
1 dessertspoon grated cheese
parsley
1 small onion

Melt a big knob of butter in a double saucepan – or a small non-stick pan. Stir in a dessertspoon of flour, moisten it with a little chicken stock or some of the milk. Gradually add the rest of the milk, stirring till you have a creamy but fairly runny sauce. Add the pieces of chicken, finely diced, and heat through gently for 5 minutes. Stir in the grated cheese and heat a little longer. Sprinkle with chopped parsley.

**Chopped Chicken Salad with Yogurt Dressing*

110 g (4 oz) cold cooked chicken
1 tomato
1 tablespoon cooked baby french beans
½ teaspoon grated onion
2 dessertspoons plain yogurt
½ teaspoon lemon juice

Peel the tomato. Chop the chicken, beans and tomato, then mash them together with a fork. Keep cool but not refrigerated – babies seldom enjoy ice-cold food. For the dressing, mix the grated onion with the yogurt and lemon juice. Dress the chicken salad *just* before you serve.

**Leftover Pie*

2 slices cold roast lamb or beef
1 large or 2 medium potatoes

milk
parsley
wheatgerm
butter

Mince or *mouli* the meat. Wash the potatoes and steam them in their skins. Skin them and transfer to a lightly-buttered casserole. Mash the potatoes with a fork, adding enough milk – warmed – to make a creamy purée. Stir in the meat with a little chopped parsley. Sprinkle the top with wheatgerm, dot with butter and bake at 190°C (375°F), gas mark 5 for 15 minutes, until it begins to brown on top.

**Spanish Monday

170 g (6 oz) cold cooked chicken
2 small cooked potatoes
¾ cup tomato juice
1 teaspoon grated onion
basil – fresh or dried
1 egg

Preheat the oven to 180°C (350°F), gas mark 4. Chop the chicken and potatoes, add tomato juice, and grated onion. Sprinkle a spot of basil. Beat egg lightly and pour over the chicken mixture. Cook in the oven for 30 minutes.

15

Eggs and Vegetables, etc.

The egg and vegetable dishes in this section are not intended simply as light snacks, or side-dishes to go with a main-order of braised beef or steak. For a small baby, almost any one of these dishes is a complete meal in itself, with enough cheese and milk or egg added to supply the protein she needs. They have the advantage of being a great deal simpler and quicker to prepare than most of the meat dishes – and cheaper into the bargain. Many of them are two-star dishes, incidentally, simply because it's not practicable to cook smaller amounts than those given, so you may as well enjoy the same delicious meal as your baby. But there is not one of them which isn't perfectly suitable for a small baby, once mashed with a fork, blended, or put through the finest sieve of your *mouli*.

Potato Cheese I

  1 medium potato
  1 teaspoon grated cheese
  milk

Boil the potato until soft, skin it, mash it, grate in the cheese, and add enough warmed milk to make a creamy purée.

*Potato Cheese II

1 medium potato
milk
1 dessertspoon cottage cheese

Boil the potato until soft, skin it, mash it with a little warmed milk, stir in the cottage cheese.

*Carrot Cloud

2 or 3 tender young carrots
butter
milk
leaf of young spinach *or* small chunk of green pepper

Scrape and finely dice the carrots, put them in a pan with just enough water to cover, and cook until they are soft – about 15 minutes. Drop them in the blender with a knob of butter, 1 dessertspoon of milk, spinach leaf or green pepper. Blend and serve.

*Cucumber Cheese

1 50-mm (2-in) chunk cucumber
parsley
cottage cheese

Pare the cucumber and if the pips are too obtrusive, cut them out. Cut the cucumber into chunks, drop them in the blender with a sprig of parsley and a dessertspoon of cottage cheese. Blend. A cool fresh dish for a hot summer day.

*Tomato Cheese

Another summertime treat, a variation on the above recipe.

  1 ripe red tomato
  cottage cheese
  parsley

Skin and de-seed the tomato, cut it in pieces, drop in the blender with a dessertspoon of cottage cheese and a sprig of parsley. Blend.

For other variations, try adding a young spinach leaf, a pale crisp lettuce leaf, or any fresh green herb.

*Potato and Carrot Cream

  1 medium carrot
  1 small potato
  butter
  milk

Scrape and dice the carrot, peel and dice the potato, put them in a small pan with a small knob of butter, and enough milk just to cover – about 150 ml (¼ pint). Simmer gently till all the liquid has boiled away – about 15 minutes – by which time the vegetables will be soft enough to mash with a fork. To make it less rich, leave out the butter.

*Turnip and Carrot Purée

  1 small turnip
  1 medium carrot

water
butter

Choose a small turnip for this: the little young ones have a milder sweeter flavour than the bigger ones. Scrape and dice the turnip, scrape and dice the carrot. Put them in a pan with 150 ml (¼ pint) water, bring to the boil, simmer for about 20 minutes – until both vegetables are soft. Mash with a dot of butter.

For variation, stir in a little grated cheese.

*Carrot and Egg

1 small carrot
1 egg
milk

Scrape and dice the carrot, put in a small pan with enough water to cover, bring to the boil and simmer gently until soft. Meanwhile, lightly boil the egg. When the carrot is cooked, mash it with a fork, extract the soft yolk from the egg, and mash it in, together with a little milk to make it into a creamy purée.

There are heaps of possible variations on this theme: add the soft egg yolk, for instance, to a teaspoon of chopped spinach, a little purée of fresh young peas, some skinned and de-seeded tomato or chunks of steamed and mashed courgette.

*Stew-Pack Dinner

If you have a freezer, stock it with a couple of those packets of mixed prepared vegetables which most supermarkets sell. All the scraping and dicing is done for you – all you need do is to extract a spoonful and seal the pack up again. Three particularly nice ones are Marks & Spencer's Mixed Vegetables – diced carrots, peas, swedes and turnip: their Stew Pack with diced carrots, celery, leeks, onions and swede: or Findus Country Mix of peas, beans, carrots, and cauliflowers. For mums in a hurry, here's how to turn them into instant lunch:

1 spoonful mixed vegetables
water

Put a dessertspoon of mixed vegetables in a small pan, add water to cover, bring to the boil and simmer gently until the vegetables are soft – 15–20 minutes. Drain – if they have not absorbed all the water. Mash. Now add one of the following: a little grated cheese, a spot of cottage cheese, a coffeespoon of wheatgerm or a little chopped fresh parsley. And that's *that* meal.

**Cottage Eggs

1 egg
butter
1 tablespoon cottage cheese (the variety with chives makes this dish prettier)

Heat the oven to 200°C (400°F), gas mark 6. Butter a small cocotte. Beat the egg. Stir it into a tablespoon of cottage cheese. Put the mixture in the cocotte and bake for 10 minutes.

Courgettes with Yogurt

2 or 3 small courgettes
butter
1 egg
2 tablespoons yogurt
1 tablespoon grated cheese

Wash the courgettes and chop into large slices, then blanch in boiling salted water for 5 minutes. Pat dry with kitchen paper and line a buttered heatproof dish with them. Beat the egg and blend into the yogurt. Add half the grated cheese. Stir well and pour the mixture over the courgettes. Sprinkle with the remaining cheese. Cook at 190°C (375°F), gas mark 5 until the top is brown – about 15 minutes.

Cottage Cheese and Spinach Soufflé

110 g (4 oz) cooked, drained spinach
4 tablespoons cottage cheese
2 egg yolks
50 g (2 oz) grated cheese
3 egg whites
butter

Chop the spinach finely and then mix it with the cottage cheese. Add the egg yolk and the grated cheese. Whisk the egg whites, fold them into the spinach mixture, and pile the lot into a small buttered casserole or two cocotte dishes. Bake at 190°C (375°F), gas mark 5 for about 35 to 40 minutes – a little less if you are using individual dishes.

**Cheese Pudding

> 2 slices bread (wholemeal or wheatgerm)
> butter
> 1 egg
> 1 cup milk
> a dash of allspice
> 3 dessertspoons grated mild Cheddar cheese

Cut the bread into squares and line a buttered heatproof dish with it. Melt a knob of butter and spoon over the bread. Mix the egg and milk together with a fork. Add the allspice and pour over the bread. Press the bread well down into the egg mixture – it tends to float to the top – sprinkle with grated cheese and cook at 190°C (375°F), gas mark 5 for 35 minutes.

**Cauliflower Puff

> ½ small cauliflower
> 1 large tomato
> butter
> 2 eggs
> milk
> 2 tablespoons grated cheese
> ¼ teaspoon dill weed

Break the cauliflower into sprigs and cut away any large lumps of stalk. Cook it in boiling water for 5 minutes only and drain. Meanwhile, skin and chop the tomato. Melt a knob of butter in a small heatproof casserole – the sort that will go on a hot plate – and soften the vegetables in it for a few minutes. Separate the eggs: beat the yolks with 1 dessertspoon of milk and half the grated cheese, and add

B.C.-D

the dill weed. Whisk the egg whites and fold into the yolk mixture. Sprinkle the cauliflower and tomato with the remaining cheese. Pile the egg mixture on top and bake for about 20 minutes at 190°C (375°F), gas mark 5.

Broccoli Cheese Scramble

1 small packet frozen or a few sprigs of fresh broccoli
butter
2 eggs
1 tablespoon grated cheese

Cook the broccoli as instructed on the packet; if it's fresh, cook in boiling water till the stalks are tender. While it's cooking, melt a knob of butter in a non-stick saucepan. Beat the eggs, stir in the grated cheese and pour the mixture on to the melted butter. Cook, stirring continuously, until it is smooth and creamy. Drain and chop the cooked broccoli, and mix into the scrambled egg. Nice with brown bread and butter fingers.

Variations: skin and chop a nice red tomato, melt it in the butter and scramble egg on top of it, stirring it in, instead of adding broccoli. Or – when there is a summer-time glut of asparagus and the thin young shoots are relatively cheap, some steamed and chopped asparagus tips.

Courgette Casserole

3 or 4 small courgettes
1 egg
1 tablespoon mild grated cheese
milk
butter
wheatgerm

Wash and slice the courgettes. Simmer them in a little water until they are tender – about 5 minutes. Drain. Mix with the beaten egg, the grated cheese and a little milk if necessary. Put in a buttered cocotte. Top with a little wheatgerm and bake in a moderate oven at 180°C (350°F), gas mark 4 for 10 minutes.

**Eggs in Onion Sauce

   1 hard-boiled egg, sliced
   a knob of butter
   1 large onion, finely chopped
   1 teaspoon wholewheat flour
   ½ cup warmed milk
   parsley
   wheatgerm

Melt the butter in a small pan. Gently fry the finely-chopped onion in it, add the flour and stir until the mixture is soft and golden. Gradually add the warmed milk. Let it cook very gently for another 10 minutes. Stir in the sliced hard-boiled egg, season with a little chopped parsley, and put in a cocotte. Top with a little wheatgerm. Slide under a hot grill for 2 or 3 minutes.

Variation: instead of onion, stir a dessertspoon of grated cheese into the sauce after you have added the milk.

**Courgettes and Cheese

   4 small courgettes
   1 dessertspoon cream or cottage cheese

Clean and finely slice the courgettes. Steam them for a couple of minutes, until they are soft. Mash them with a fork. Serve with a big spoonful of cream or cottage cheese on top.

**Eggy Spinach*

1 small packet frozen spinach
butter
1 egg
1 dessertspoon cottage cheese

Heat the oven to about 180°C (350°F), gas mark 4. Thaw a small packet of frozen spinach. When it is softened, spoon it into a buttered cocotte. Make a hole in the middle and break into it one egg – two if you are both feeling hungry! Cover with the cottage cheese. Bake for 15 minutes.

Variation: Use grated cheese to cover instead of cottage cheese or sprinkle with wheatgerm or brown breadcrumbs and dot with butter.

**Vegetable Casserole*

3 new potatoes
2 small tomatoes
4 small carrots
1 slice onion
butter
3 tablespoons chicken stock or water
parsley

Heat the oven to about 180°C (350°F), gas mark 4. Clean and slice the potatoes; skin and chop the tomatoes; scrape and slice the carrots, and chop the onion. Butter a small casserole and put the vegetables in with the stock, if you have it, or with plain water. Cover the casserole and bake in the oven for 1 hour.

Cheesy Jacket Potatoes

    2 medium potatoes
    butter
    2 eggs
    1 tablespoon grated Cheddar cheese

Heat the oven to 180°C (350°F), gas mark 4, and bake the potatoes till they are done – about 45 minutes. Then halve the potatoes, scoop out the flesh, mash it with a knob of butter. Beat the eggs and stir into the potato, add the grated cheese and mix until all the ingredients are blended. Heat the grill. Divide the mixture into four portions, and pile them into the four potato halves. Grill until they are golden brown.

Potato and Tomato Casserole

    2 medium potatoes
    2 large ripe tomatoes
    butter
    1 tablespoon grated cheese
    basil – fresh or dried
    milk
    wheatgerm

Steam the potatoes till they are cooked, skin, and slice.
Skin and slice the tomatoes. Butter a small casserole, fill it
with layers of potato, tomato and grated cheese. If you
have a little fresh or dried basil, add it. Pour in 1
tablespoon of milk. Top with wheatgerm, dot with butter,
and bake in a moderate oven at 180°C (350°F), gas mark 4
for about 25 minutes.

**Watercress and Cheese Spread

   1 tablespoon watercress
   50 g (2 oz) cream cheese
   1 teaspoon sour cream
   dash of horseradish sauce
   ¼ teaspoon grated onion

Separate the watercress into sprigs. Remove most of the
stalks. Chop the remainder finely. Beat the cream cheese,
sour cream and horseradish sauce together. Add the
grated onion and the chopped watercress. Mix well.
Spread on brown bread for tea.

**Carrot Salad

   2 medium carrots
   vegetable oil
   cottage cheese
   a little lemon juice
   chives

Shred or grate the scraped carrots very finely. Put them in
a little china dish and stir in a teaspoon of vegetable oil, 1

tablespoon cottage cheese, and a dash of fresh lemon
juice. Garnish with chopped chives.

**Tomato Salad

> 2 ripe tomatoes
> vegetable oil
> yogurt
> lemon juice
> parsley

Skin and slice the tomatoes. Put a dessertspoon each of
vegetable oil and plain yogurt in the blender with a dash of
freshly squeezed lemon juice, and a sprig of parsley.
Blend. Pour over the tomatoes.

Variation: use cottage cheese instead of yogurt.

16
Tea-time Treats

For small babies, much the best and most valuable way to serve them fruit is fresh, ripe and uncooked: on its own for the clean good taste; or served with yogurt or cottage cheese to make a baby-sized square meal out of it; or grated into their very own muesli (see recipe p. 110). Later on, hungry toddlers need a little more variety at mealtimes, and what's nicer for nursery tea, on a cold wintry afternoon, than a spicy apple crumble? So I have also included recipes for a few hot fruit puddings, as well as a simplified version of that wonderful summer time treat for grown-ups – Summer Pudding. And for a change, there's a group of fresh fruit blender drinks which – enriched with nuts, yeast or yogurt – are almost a meal in themselves. None of these recipes contains added sugar, although in one or two cases I have suggested sweetening with a little honey. A *very* little. Don't give honey to babies under about 9 months, though; there could be a faint risk of botulism, according to US experts.

*Ripe Banana

Mash a ripe banana with a little yogurt, a spurt of fresh lemon or orange juice, perhaps a speck of nutmeg. Or try cottage cheese instead of yogurt.

*Squashy Ripe Pear

Mash a very ripe pear, and grate into it a little very soft apple.

*Crisp Apple

Wash but do not peel a crisp apple, then put chunks in the blender with a little cottage cheese and a dash of lemon juice and blend. For a change, add a couple of seedless raisins to the blender; or a little flaked almond.

*Ripe Peach

Skin a ripe peach and put in the blender with a teaspoon of yogurt, or serve on its own.

**Favourite Baked Apple

    1 large apple (Bramleys are best for baking)
    4 or 5 dried apricots or a few sultanas
    honey
    butter
    cinnamon
    nutmeg

Pour boiling water over the apricots if you are including them, and leave them to soften for an hour or so. When you are ready to prepare the apple, chop the apricots. Core the apple – but remember not to pierce the skin at the bottom end, or all the filling will drop out – then stuff it with the apricots or sultanas, and a teaspoon of honey. Rub the apple with a little softened butter, sprinkle it with a little cinnamon and nutmeg, then stand it in a small buttered baking tin: bake in a moderate oven at 180°C (350°F), gas mark 4 for about 25 minutes.

Rice Cream

1 scant tablespoon brown rice
½ cup milk
1 teaspoon honey
1 strip of lemon peel
nutmeg, cinnamon
A few raisins, if liked

Heat the oven to 150°C (300°F), gas mark 2. Wash the
rice, put it in a small casserole, add the milk – it should
more than cover the rice – stir in the honey, add the lemon
peel and a dash of nutmeg or cinnamon. Cover tightly and
bake for about 50 minutes or 1 hour. For a change, use
orange peel instead of the lemon; or serve it cold with a
teaspoonful of orange juice and a dollop of yogurt stirred
in. If you like, a few raisins can be added to the rice before
cooking.

Baked Egg Custard

1 egg
a little honey
½ cup warmed milk
nutmeg

Beat the egg lightly with the honey, add the warmed milk
and a dash of nutmeg, pour into two small buttered
cocotte dishes. Bake in a cool oven at 150°C (300°F), gas
mark 2 for 45 minutes. This pudding must not boil or the
egg will curdle. It can be eaten hot or cold.

**Hot Cottage Plums

3 ripe Victoria plums
1 tablespoon cottage cheese
a little honey
1 egg
1 teaspoon condensed milk.

Stew the plums lightly. Remove skins and stones. Mash the pulp with a fork. Whisk the cottage cheese, egg and condensed milk together till creamy. Stir in plum pulp and spoon into a small buttered heatproof dish. Cook at 180°C (350°F), gas mark 4 until set – about 45 minutes.

**Apple Crumble

1 large Bramley apple
butter
lemon juice
1 tablespoon oats
wheatgerm
a little honey
pinch of cinnamon

Wash and slice the apple, and put the slices into a buttered cocotte dish. Heat the oven to 180°C (350°F), gas mark 4 and put in the apples to start cooking. Sprinkle with lemon juice. Make the crumble by mixing the oats, about a teaspoon of wheatgerm, a little honey, the cinnamon and a knob of butter together. Spread over the top of the apples and bake until the top is crisp and golden.

**Prune and Apricot Crumble

8–10 dried apricots and prunes
1 teaspoon orange juice
a little grated nutmeg
1 tablespoon wholewheat flour and muesli, mixed
a knob of butter

Wash the fruit and soak it overnight in a cupful of boiling water. Next day, bring fruit and water to the boil, and simmer till tender. Stone the prunes, and put the fruit into a small casserole, stirring in the orange juice and nutmeg. Mix the flour, muesli and butter – it should look soft and crumbly – and spread on top of the fruit. Bake at 180°C (350°F), gas mark 4 until the top is nicely gilded – about half an hour.

**Summer Pudding

2 slices wholemeal bread
1 tablespoon strawberries (those cheap squashy ones they almost give away in midsummer will do splendidly – and a few raspberries too if possible)
yogurt or cream

Cut the crusts off the bread and line a little basin with them – a small cup would do. Put the strawberries and raspberries in a pan over a very gentle heat – they don't need water – and let them stew until the juice runs (3 or 4 minutes). Then turn them out into the little bread-lined basin – they should fill it to the top – cover with another little slice of bread, put a plate with a weight on top and leave in the fridge for at least a few hours, preferably overnight. Turn out the lovely purply mould, and serve with cool fresh plain yogurt, or a little cream.

**Apricot Whip

2 tablespoons dried apricots
1 teaspoon brewers' yeast
2 tablespoons yogurt
1 cup milk

Pour boiling water over the apricots and leave them to soften for an hour or so. Put all the ingredients in the blender, whizz for a couple of minutes. A meal in a drink.

**Apple Froth

1 small apple, washed, and cored and quartered.
1 dessertspoon cottage cheese or 1 dessertspoon yogurt
1 squeeze lemon juice
1 dessertspoon milk

Blend all the ingredients together.

**Saturday Special

1 small apple, cored but unpeeled
1 teaspoon mixed nuts
1 small cup milk
2 dessertspoons yogurt
½ teaspoon brewers' yeast

Put all the ingredients in the blender and whizz.

**Bibi's High-Protein Special

1 banana
1 dessertspoon brewers' yeast

300 ml (½ pint) milk
1 140 g (5 oz) carton yogurt

Put all the ingredients in a blender and whizz. Enough for
2 big glasses – each one a meal in itself. Great for little
boys and girls who need building up after a nasty cold – it
is packed with iron and protein – but can't face a proper
meal.

**Do-it-Yourself Yogurt*

Store-bought yogurt is reasonably cheap – around £1 for a
whole kilo of the stuff, last time I looked – so making your
own is not much of an economy, unless you suddenly find
you have got a glut of milk to dispose of. Here's one way
of using it up. Heat 600 ml (1 pint) of milk to blood-heat –
do not boil – and whisk in a dessertspoon of a nice firm
proprietary yogurt (Eden Vale is good for this). Cover the
basin with a folded clean tea-cloth and let it stand for 6–8
hours in a warm, dry, draught-free place; not *too* warm,
though. An airing-cupboard is splendid; or the oven, with
just the pilot light left on, or the warm drawer beneath it.
When it is set, uncover it and put in the fridge. It will
thicken up even more. This makes a particularly pleasant,
light, creamy yogurt, and even if it's not an economy, it's a
nice change from the bought kind.

**Baby's Own Muesli*

The grinder part of your blender is perfect for this. Put in
a couple of tablespoons of flaked oats, a teaspoon of
wheatgerm – to give your baby iron – and grind to a

powder. To serve, simply soak it in a little milk or fruit juice for a few minutes. For variety, grind a few sultanas with it, or some nuts; and serve it with fresh apple or pear grated into it.

17

A Week's Menu for a 6-month-old Baby

	Sunday	Monday	Tuesday	Wednesday	Thursday	Friday	Saturday
10 A.M.	Banana mashed with yogurt and a little fresh orange juice	The yolk of a boiled egg with fingers of wholewheat bread soaked in milk	*Muesli with grated fresh apple	Banana mashed with yogurt and a little wheatgerm	*Muesli with fresh pear grated into it and a little yogurt	Banana mashed with yogurt and a little wheatgerm	Yolk of boiled egg, with fingers of wholewheat bread soaked in milk
2 A.M.	*Chicken Liver Treat	*Turnip and Carrot purée. Grated ripe pear with orange juice	Spinach purée with cottage cheese. A little mashed banana	*Braised Liver with boiled potato. *Tomato cheese	*Potato and Carrot cream. Grated ripe fresh pear with a little orange juice	*Fish cream. Grated ripe pear	*Chicken and Tomato I. Stewed apricots blended with a little yogurt
6 P.M.	*Potato cheese II. Grated fresh apple	Stewed apricots blended with yogurt and a little lemon juice	*Carrot and potato soup	The yolk of a boiled egg, with fingers of wholewheat bread soaked in milk	Stewed apple with yogurt, fingers of wholewheat bread and butter soaked in milk	*Muesli with grated fresh apple and yogurt	Mashed banana with orange juice

Starred dishes are made from recipes in this book.

A Week's Menu for an 18-month-old Baby

	Sunday	Monday	Tuesday	Wednesday	Thursday	Friday	Saturday
Breakfast	Scrambled egg with fingers of wholewheat bread	*Muesli with yogurt and grated apple	Fingers of buttered wholewheat bread with cheese	*Muesli with yogurt and apple grated into it	Boiled egg with fingers of buttered wholewheat bread	*Muesli with yogurt and banana	Boiled egg with fingers of buttered wholewheat toast
Lunch	**Poached chicken – served from the family lunch	**Cottage eggs. Fresh ripe pear	**Greased Lightning casserole. **Carrot salad	**Eggs in onion sauce. Fresh ripe pear	**Cod in cheese sauce. Grated raw apple	**Baked liver and onion **Tomato salad	**Courgette casserole. Fingers of carrot and cucumber
Supper	Baked potato mashed with butter and cottage cheese. Fresh apple	**Favourite baked apple. Fingers of buttered wholewheat bread and cheese	*Scrambled Roe served with finger of buttered wholewheat bread. Banana	**Tomato soup. Fingers of buttered wholewheat toast	Baked potato mashed with cottage cheese. Fingers of cucumber and raw carrot	**Apple crumble with yogurt	**Apple froth. Fingers of wholewheat bread with cheese

Starred dishes are made from recipes in this book.

The Important Nutrients
and which foods supply them

The foods listed here are not the only source of each particular nutrient, but they are readily available, and they are all suited to baby eating. They are printed in descending order of importance: thus, blackcurrants are the best known source of Vitamin C, and duly occupy the place of honour at the top of the list. But there are still useful amounts of this indispensable vitamin in potatoes, at the bottom of the list.

VITAMIN A
Essential for growth, and the body's defences against infection; ensures good eyesight.
Sources: liver and fish-oils, carrots, apricots, milk and dairy products, fresh green vegetables, especially spinach. The vitamin is gradually destroyed by cooking.

THE B VITAMINS
Essential for growth, good digestion, clear skin, the health of the nervous system, resistance to stress, and learning ability.
Sources: brewers' yeast, wheatgerm, liver, wholegrain cereals, yogurt, green vegetables (cooked without bicarbonate of soda, please).

VITAMIN C
Essential for protection against infection and stress – the body's marvellous immune system can't function properly

without it – for building healthy teeth and bones, for general well-being.
Sources: blackcurrants, citrus fruit, tomatoes, red and green peppers, raw green vegetables, fresh fruit, potatoes. Vitamin C is destroyed by cooking and exposure to air: don't press oranges or cut up vegetables till the last possible moment.

VITAMIN D
Essential for building healthy bones and teeth.
Sources: Much the best source is sunlight (the important bits of which get through even on quite cloudy days) which is why your baby's daily airing is so important: fish-liver oils are the only other dependable source, although it's also found in minute quantities in egg yolk and milk. So make sure your baby has either cod-liver oil, in liquid or capsule form, or one of the A, D, & C droplet preparations: since baby-formulas as usually supplemented, this may only be necessary once she starts on cow's milk.

VITAMIN E
Essential for healthy cells and a healthy vascular system: regulates the body's supply of oxygen.
Sources: vegetable oils, nuts, fresh wheatgerm, stone-ground wholemeal flour, avocados.

PROTEIN
Protein is what growing babies are made of: they need it to build and nourish skin, tissues, muscles.
Sources: chicken, meat, fish, eggs, milk, cheese, yogurt, cottage cheese.

FATS

Essential in small amounts for the normal functioning of the body.

Sources: natural vegetable oils, nuts, milk, butter, cheese.

MINERALS

At least 20 different minerals are found in a healthy functioning body, some in such minute amounts that they are known as trace elements. Some of them, like iron and calcium, have been studied for years: the vital importance of others – such as zinc and manganese – is only just becoming evident. Most of them are found in wholegrain cereals, fruit, vegetables – and much of them is daily chucked away all over the country along with the peelings, and the water in which they were cooked, while impressive quantities are milled out of flour when it is refined. Some of the most important: CALCIUM, needed to build bones and teeth – by far the best source is milk and dairy products; IRON, essential for good healthy red blood: liver, wheatgerm and brewers' yeast, wholegrain cereal, apricot, egg yolks, fresh green vegetables; MAGNESIUM: essential for healthy nerves and muscle function; found in milk, nuts, wholegrains, eggs, dark green vegetables. Most of the exciting research on ZINC has been done within the last decade: we now know that it's vital for growth, development, and healthy brain function, to list just some of its functions. It also helps protect against the uptake of toxic metals like lead and cadmium, increasingly found in our environment. Best sources of zinc are wheatgerm, sunflower seeds, eggs, brewers' yeast. SODIUM – but what you want to watch out for, in this case, is excess: too much sodium can cause high blood pressure and other problems. So use no salt when cooking for your baby – remember that it's found in a lot of everyday processed foods such as stock-cubes – and try and bring your baby up without either a sweet or a salt tooth!

20
Some Useful Addresses

If you have any problem with breast-feeding, contact the National Childbirth Trust, who will put you in touch with a breast-feeding counsellor in your area. Look in your telephone directory to see if they have a branch locally. If so, it's well worth joining for educational and social contact with other new mothers, practical help with post-natal problems, and general moral support; otherwise contact their head office:

> 9 Queensborough Terrace,
> London W2 3TB
> Tel: 01 221 3833

If you suspect that your child is suffering from an allergic problem, and your GP or Child Clinic is unhelpful, the British Society for Clinical Ecology is an association of doctors trained to cope with allergy and sensitivity problems. Write to the Secretary for the address of a doctor in your area that you could contact:

Secretary: Dr Ronald Finn, MD FRCP, Consultant
          Physician,
          Royal Liverpool Hospital,
          Prescot Street,
          Liverpool L7 8XP

If you would like to know more about allergies, how they arise and how to cope with them, join Action Against Allergy, started by a woman who herself battled with ill health problems arising from multiple allergies for years before her problem was diagnosed. A year's subscription is £5. Their address is:

> Action Against Allergy,
> 43 The Downs,
> London SW20 8HG

And more practical advice, contacts with similar sufferers, and general information is offered by the National Society for Research into Allergy. Ordinary membership £3.00 per annum.

> National Society for Research into Allergy,
> P.O.Box No. 45,
> Hinckley,
> Leicestershire, LE10 IJY

If your baby cries for hours on end, sleeps ten minutes instead of right through the night, is restless and fretful, doesn't like to be cuddled, and generally behaves quite unlike a normal, contented cuddly little baby, it could be that she's sensitive to something in her diet. The Hyperactive Children's Support Group deal with thousands of enquiries annually from bewildered, exhausted parents, promotes research into problems of this kind, and will put you in touch with a local group where you can swop notes with parents who have the same problem. Membership is £3 annually.

Secretary: Mrs Sally Bunday
> 59 Meadowside,
> Angmering,
> West Sussex

Please send a stamped addressed envelope with your enquiry when you write to any of these groups.

International Conversion Tables

The weights and measures used throughout this book are based on British Imperial standards and metric. However, the following tables show you how to convert the various weights and measures simply.

International Measures

Measure	UK	Australia	New Zealand	Canada	USA
1 pint	20 *fl oz*	20 *fl oz*	20 *fl oz*	20 *fl oz*	16 *fl oz*
1 cup	10 *fl oz*	8 *fl oz*	8 *fl oz*	8 *fl oz*	8 *fl oz*
1 tablespoon	⅝ *fl oz*	½ *fl oz*	½ *fl oz*	½ *fl oz*	½ *fl oz*
1 dessertspoon	⅖ *fl oz*	no official measure	—	—	—
1 teaspoon	⅕ *fl oz*	⅛ *fl oz*	⅙ *fl oz*	⅙ *fl oz*	⅛ *fl oz*
1 gill	5 *fl oz*	—	—	—	—

Conversion of fluid ounces to metric

1 *fl oz*	= 2.84 *ml*
35 *fl oz* (approx 1¾ Imperial pints)	= 1 litre (1000 ml or 10 *decilitres*)
1 Imperial pint (20 *fl oz*)	= 600 *ml* (6 *dl*)
½ Imperial pint (10 *fl oz*)	= 300 *ml* (3 *dl*)
¼ Imperial pint (5 *fl oz*)	= 150 *ml* (1½ *dl*)
4 tablespoons (2½ *fl oz*)	= 70 *ml* (7 *cl*)
2 tablespoons (1¼ *fl oz*)	= 35 *ml* (3½ *cl*)
1 tablespoon (⅝ *fl oz*)	= 18 *ml* (2 *cl*)
1 dessertspoon (⅖ *fl oz*)	= 12 *ml*
1 teaspoon (⅕ *fl oz*)	= 6 *ml*

(All the above metric equivalents are approximate)

Conversion of solid weights to metric

2 *lb* 3 *oz* = 1*kg* (*kilogramme*)
1 *lb*   = 450 *g* (*grammes*)
12 *oz*   = 339 *g*
8 *oz*   = 225 *g*
4 *oz*   = 110 *g*
2 *oz*   = 56 *g*
1 *oz*   = 25 *g*

US Equivalents

In converting American recipes for metric or Imperial use, note that the US pint is 16 *fl oz* (454.6 *ml*) against the Imperial pint of 20 *fl oz* (568.3 *ml*). Americans tend to use cups (8 *fl oz*) for measuring quantities of solids, like flour, beans, raisins, even chopped vegetables. If you own a number of American recipe books, invest in a US cup measure as well.

Oven temperatures

Description	Electric Setting	Gas Mark
Very cool	225°F (110°C)	¼
	250°F (130°C)	½
Cool	275°F (140°C)	1
	300°F (150°C)	2
Very moderate	325°F (170°C)	3
Moderate	350°F (180°C)	4
Moderately or	375°F (190°C)	5
fairly hot	400°F (200°C)	6
Hot	425°F (220°C)	7
	450°F (230°C)	8
Very hot	475°F (240°C)	9

These temperatures are only an approximate guide as all ovens vary slightly, acccording to the make and country of manufacture.

Index

Cooking for good health books now available in Panther Books

Ursula Gruniger
Cooking with Fruit   50p ☐

Sheila Howarth
Grow, Freeze and Cook   £1.50 ☐

Kenneth Lo
Cooking and Eating the Chinese Way   £1.50 ☐
The Wok Cookbook   £1.50 ☐

L D Michaels
The Complete Book of Pressure Cooking   £1.25 ☐

Franny Singer
The Slow Crock Cookbook   £1.50 ☐

Janet Walker
Vegetarian Cookery   £1.50 ☐

Beryl Wood
Let's Preserve It   £1.50 ☐

Gretel Beer and Paula Davies
The Diabetic Gourmet   75p ☐

David Scott
The Japanese Cookbook   £1.50 ☐

Marika Hanbury Tenison
Cooking with Vegetables   £1.95 ☐

Pamela Westland
Bean Feast   £1.50 ☐
High-Fibre Vegetarian Cookery   £1.95 ☐

To order direct from the publisher just tick the titles you want and fill in the order form.